Get the Monkey Off Your Back

An Odyssey of Self-Discovery

By Marilyn Richard

Dedication

I dedicate the book to all the mothers who did the best they could and to all the fathers to let them know that they are needed, and to the children you will forever be loved by your Heavenly Father.

FORWARD

Get the Monkey Off You Back was a journey to accomplish. This story has caused me to open my eyes as to what God has for me. This story is based on my mother's life. She has been through many ups and downs but through it all, she overcame and broke through barriers that most people would have given up on. God was merciful in her life and as you read this book, you will begin to identify your own personal monkeys. You will be able to recognize that God is no respecter of persons, meaning that what He has done in someone elses life, he can do that and more for you.

I was a child when the events of this book were unfolding. I was shielded from a great deal of things that could have altered my life in ways that I could not have imagined. My mother taught me how to be a mother. She taught me through action how to be a lady. She is my role model. Her story is one of triumph and perseverance. She covers many topics such as drug abuse, molestation, domestic violence, a lesbian encounter and death. The tribulations that she walked through helped her to become the strong woman that she is today.

The events in this book should be used to examine your own life. Monkeys are metaphorical creatures that sit on your back and weigh you down. They cause you to stumble. You have to be strong to overcome them and say, "I will survive. This will not beat me."

I pray that this book is as much a blessing to you as it was for me. I, too, have identified my own monkeys and I am kicking them off my back as soon as they pop up. God bless all who read this literary work and are empowered by the words therein.

Forever Your Daughter,

Candace Farria.

Preface

My name is Marilyn and I discovered a problem that is destroying lives. I call it the monkey. The monkey is any negative feeling that causes you to be destructive: a feeling of shame, low self-esteem, embarrassment, hatred, jealously, fear, resentment, and pain. I think you can get an idea of where I am going with this.

I invite you on a journey into my life where I discovered the source of my pain and how I got the monkey off of my back.

It was April 2010 and I walked into the office determined to be very open. My hair was in place; my posture was straight and strong. My clothing fit me to my satisfaction. In my mind, I was well put together. I was determined to greet the receptionist behind the window with a smile on my face and prayed that the pain behind my eyes was not showing. To my relief, no one was at the desk. There was however, a clipboard propped against the sliding glass window with a note. *To be completed for the twelve o'clock appointment.* Following the instructions, I took the clipboard, had a seat and proceeded to tell the truth and only the truth. Name, address, and insurance information, that was easy enough. I turned the page to medical history and all I saw was question after question of what have I been through. I realized it was time to tell the truth the story of my life. I was determined to tell my story in hopes to stop the secret pain that I have held for forty years.

It all begins when I was eight and the death of my father. I remembered a strong man. I sat there smile on my face while watching him shave. He stood in front of the mirror, wearing an "A" shirt now called *wife beaters*. It is funny how a moment of comfort becomes distorted by a name given to a shirt. I quickly removed the thought of domestic violence and returned to the bathroom where my father was shaving. In the background, there is country music playing and I watched my father apply shaving cream to his face. He turned to me put some cream on my nose and I remember giggling as I wiped it off. I watched him with his precise movement to get a smooth shave. I looked at the waves in his hair and watched his arm as he dragged the blade forward from his neck. Looking back, I realized how the strokes of the razor going across his face were well thought out and was not random at all. Shaving line by line, until all the cream was gone. I remember the water running in the sink to rinse the razor occasionally.

My mind goes to water. Oh, how much water comforts me. Lakes, waterfalls, beaches, the crashing of waves and even water running in the sink all make me happy. Sitting in my therapist's office, I realized why I love water. It all began with a shave. My mind quickly returns to the green liquid in the bottle on top of the medicine cabinet. *My father picks up the bottle and shook some in his hands then winced as he put his hands to his face. I would look at the bottle the caused my dad to inhale to take the momentary discomfort and the exhale to receive the cooling feeling of Mennen after-shave. He then picked me up and twirled me around. It was a ritual of ours.* It was the safest moment in my life and a bond that my dad and I shared.

Next question. I tensed while dragging the

pen on the paper. Parents: living or deceased. I was proud that my mother was eighty-six and still thriving with good health. She had a strength about her and I was glad to inherit that quality. The more I thought about my mother, the lonelier I became. I began thinking of the friends I have and the number of relationships I have acquired over my years on this earth and I cannot think of many. I have siblings but we are not even close. I realized that I had inherited more than just strength from my mother but a shield to avoid getting hurt. I now sit in this waiting room alone because of that shield answering questions about me and wondering who I am.

As I look around the room, I start to feel the feeling that got me here. I want to retreat but I remember that I must be honest with myself and ask the important question. Why don't I have friends? The shield of protection left me distant and in pain. The pain is so intense, but I must not complain. *Deal with it and do not allow yourself to be weak.* I thought a lot that has been done to me while I continue to complete forms that yelled out questions. *What wrong with you? Why are you here?* The answer is I do not know that is why I am in this office. *Why am I in this office?* I thought. Oh yeah, I hate people. They get on my nerves and say the most idiotic things. *Oh Marilyn that is not good, you need help.*

The therapist opens the door and greets me and I put on the winning smile while again praying that the pain does not show. I thought, *what an idiot of course she sees your pain; she is a trained professional.* I approached her with my hand extended to offer a firm yet feminine handshake. I thought of not giving the wrong impression. Many have told me that I am mean, argumentative and rude but I cannot see it. My thoughts as I walk through the door I chant to myself. *Please see me for who I am.*

I quickly noticed my surroundings. Comfortable, welcoming and *ooh she has toys!* The child within me wants to come out and play. I feel safe and am now prepared to be honest with my therapist and myself. I have been told that I take over conversations and I promised myself that I would be an active listener and get the problem resolved. The problem. What is the problem? Oh, don't you remember? You hate people. *No, no, no, I do not hate people, but I feel that some people hate me.* I sit in a therapist's office for that reason alone.

I sat on the lumpy but comfortable loveseat flashing the winning smile with eyes pleading for the pain to go away. The therapist began her introduction and asked me what could she help me with. Without control, I began to talk about my childhood. *Please see me for who I really am.*

I stated, "I am here because my daughter stated that I have a problem, that I will not let people in my life unless I can control the situation. I want to prove her wrong or get help. Help!"

I explained that I have been off work for two and half months because of a flare up of my condition, lupus, and am having anxiety attacks from the thought of returning to work. My heart races and I am starting to feel flushed and hot. I wondered why it feels as if a boot was in my chest.

Without fear, I told the story of an incident that happen at my office. The lies. I cannot get over the lies. I have no trust in a liar. Deep in my soul, a pain and then guilt wounded my spirit. Pain. Why should I have pain? I am child of God, I know of his love, and I love him. Yes People, him. Why so much pain? Please help me. All these thoughts are racing through my mind and I got off track.

Chapter 1

A typical day at the office, 8 AM. I came into the office as usual, speaking to everyone I see.

"Good Morning. Good morning", I say cheerfully until I arrived at my desk. As I sat, I thought *oh my desk.* I love my desk where I encouraged people to dream. After I turn on my computer and it hums to life, I grab my coffee cup and head for the break room for a fresh cup of Jo (My first of many). More "Good mornings" with that winning smile on the way. *I love my job and it shows* I thought.

Dumb question number one.

"Why are you so happy?" A coworker asked.

I inhaled and exhaled to show the obvious.

"I'm alive. I'm having a good day, all is well and I love my job." The coworker scoffs and I continued walking to the break room. I saw that the sink was dirty as usual and proceeded to clean it up. Another coworker entered the break room and complained about the condition of the sink then dropped a napkin on the floor and left it there. *Oh, that is pathetic* I thought as I picked it up. I hurried to wash my cup while remembering a time when I used to washed my cup before I left for the day but lately, I had been feeling more fatigued by the end of day. I got my coffee and went back to my cubicle. I thought I was doing a good job of not letting the attitudes of negative people get to me. I was proud of that.

My cubicle is located in the center of the office and is considered a high traffic area. The majority of the people spoke to me often commenting *Oh I love your shoes* or *Nice hairdo* or *Girllll you lost some weight.* Some coworkers I considered friends at the office, meaning we talked about personal issues and such, but never socialize outside the office. I had the printer and the copier not far from me and I was not in the hub of my coworkers. I liked the solitude.

I often interviewed people who had no clue of what they wanted to do to make a living towards self-sufficiency and an abundant life. They depended on government assistance as if it was a rite of passage or that it was *owed* to them. *No, no, no you have to work for this* I thought. I would encourage them to look to their future and work with them to come up with a plan to fulfill their goals. Most of the clients were grateful while others fought the program's ideas. I dealt with fear, denial, resentment and remorse of clients who felt stuck with no way out. I became the dream maker to many and someone to reckon with to others. Every letter that I sent to clients was more like an invitation not an appointment. What I found out is that most of the clients never bothered to read the letter. Why, what and when to come to see me was addressed and often they would come to the office unprepared. I took time with each person that I interviewed to ease the tension and to gain a rapport. In other words, I cared.

Forty-eight years I was happy with my life, but I felt that something was missing. People would just start talking to me. I had no problem talking to anyone as long as they did not invade my space, which was rare. Often strangers would talk about personal issues and ask for advice and I thought it was weird but I would listen intently and then advise them, as I would want to be given advice. My newfound purpose in life was developing and I had no clue of what was going on. People told me I made them happy and they often said they appreciated my time. I was happy to be good company and to see a smile on their faces after the conversation was over.

Chapter 2

My life was not all pleasant for the most part. I had struggles like everyone else. As I previously stated, my dad died when I was eight, my mom had an aneurysm when I was ten. I have endured domestic violence, been threatened with sexual abuse, drug addiction and betrayal. Through all that, I am still standing. My mother was hospitalized for about two months and I was passed around to several difference homes. I had three siblings who were already living on their own and for whatever reason I did not go to live with them. I did go to my maternal grandmother, who criticized me for the way I eat, my table manners and the way I spoke. After a week, I was handed off to my Aunt and her family where I was compared to their children and I never measured up. I remember they had given my hand me down clothes and I was so grateful and I thought they were pretty only to be told by my cousins that they wouldn't be caught dead in those clothes and that they were going to be thrown out until I came. I began to shrink with all the negative feeling that I had about myself. I did not have underwear. No one provided those things for me and now my mother was taken from me and I did not know if she was coming back.

I went to my sister Deidra's house next and that did not last long at all. I did not realize that her husband was possessive and was beating her.

Next, it was my grandfather and my step grandmother, who came to get me from San Bernardino CA. On the way back to their home, they took me to the store, The Harris CO., and bought me a wardrobe. Pretty dresses, shiny shoes and even gloves and purses. I felt like a princess. After the shopping spree, they went and bought ice cream in many flavors. I had never been treated this well and I wondered where had they been. We finally got to the house, which was big, and it was on a lot of land. I was in awe with the money that was spent and the treatment that I was receiving. I felt like they could see me for who I am and didn't judge me. I felt safe.

The security was short lived when my grandfather asked me if I wanted some ice cream. What kid didn't want ice cream? He told me to go to the pantry where the freezer was to get it. The pantry didn't have a light in it so I used the light from the kitchen. As I was deciding what flavor to choose, I noticed that the light became dim. I turn to see my grandfather tall figure standing in the doorway. I couldn't see his face, but I felt his intentions. I began to say I would tell repeatedly. He told me to get out of there. I went to bed without the ice cream and was scared to go to sleep. I didn't feel safe anymore even though there was a double-barreled shotgun prompt against the wall in the corner in the room. I didn't know what to do and I had no one to call. I felt trapped at the tender age of ten. The fear was overwhelming and all I wanted was my mother.

The morning came and my grandfather gave me a duck. I thought everything was all right but he would yell at me and I quickly learned to stay out of his way. I would be with my step grandmother snapping green beans in the kitchen and making biscuits. I enjoyed being with her until an associate of my grandfather passed by the kitchen window one day. My grandmother went to talk to him through the window. She raised her dressed, pressed her "special place" up against the window, and started to laugh. *Now that's just nasty.* I wondered what I came too. I was very quiet and full of thought. Now I had to watch her and my grandfather. I made myself scarce and played with my duck. I would tell my duck how I felt and that I was scared and I wanted to go home.

The carpenter was safer than my own family. He would come and do work on the property and I would learn how to shave wood for the cabinets, I learned about leveling and how to use the tools. Every morning, I would take care of Tilly, my duck, then dash across the yard to the building where the carpenter was.

My grandfather would stare at me as if he was mad that I didn't let him have his way and I didn't care. My grandfather used to look at me as if I was lunch, but he never ordered off the menu. *THANK GOD.* I refused to be a victim and I was terrified of being violated so I spoke up and told him, I would tell. He didn't touch me but he would do mental things like have my step grandmother cook my pet duck and serve it to me for dinner.

One morning, I couldn't find Tilly and I wondered where she could have gone. I figured she would show up eventually and went to help the carpenter. I was devastated at dinner when I was asked by my grandfather a sick question. How did I like the duck? He had a sinister look on his face. I realized that I was eating Tilly, my pet and I throw up all over the table. I was through; I couldn't take it no more. What kind of people were these? Why me? What did I do to deserve this? I cried for several days and wouldn't come out of the room.

They finally told me I was going home and I began to pack. They took everything that they had bought me and I left as I came with nothing. Later, I found out that my mother woke up from her coma and asked where I was and when she was told she became hysterical. She knew what kind of man her father was and she knew I was in danger. She would not calm down until I was taken to the hospital so she could see for herself that I was safe. I knew that my mother loved me and I knew what she must have been gone through growing up with that man. This man was the man that took his four children while his wife was at church. He raised my mother and my mother raised me.

Next I went to my older sister's, Melanie, home. She was married to daddy Clyde. He was a heroin addict and violently abusive to Melanie. One night while I was sleep he came to my bedroom and woke me up. He told me that he wanted me to braid his hair. I didn't want to do it but I was scared to say no. I didn't want what Melanie had gotten many times before, so I got up. I place a chair in the middle of the floor and he told me we wouldn't need it. He told me to sit down and when I did, he opened my legs and sat down. I was mortified and began to braid his hair with a quickness. I was trying to hurry up and get this man off of my legs when he opened up a pornography magazine and started looking at the pictures. At first I didn't know what he was reading until I saw the picture of a male member with sperm dripping down the shaft. I braided like I was trying to beat a record. Done! I told him as I tried to push him from between my legs. He turned and said I was his favorite sister in law and tried to kiss me. My look said *Nigga please* and my fear became anger. That's nasty. This old ass nigga trying to order off the menu and my sister was in the next room. I stayed up the rest of the night and was out the door at daybreak I chanted as a child. *I will live like I want when I am grown, I will live like I want when I am grown.* I didn't know that my chant was going to come with criticism.

Chapter 3

At the age of ten, I felt *homeless* with a roof over my head. I did get one meal a day unless it was a school day and then I would get three. I was alone even thought I had eight siblings. I never had family day or bonding. My mom mentioned one day that when I was a child, after she returned from the hospital I asked her, "What did they do with your brain?" I probably asked that because there was no parental authority when she came back.

I often went without basic needs like bras and panties. I would wear a bathing suit that was given to me by my friend. When I was twelve, my friend's mother bought me my first bra. It was a 36C. I cried and she was puzzle by my reaction. I explained that I appreciated the gift but it hurt because it should have been my mother. I remember in my childhood, my mother purchased a Red Spider convertible. The purchase of the car was after the gift of the bra and I felt like I was not valued.

Later that year, I was home alone which was a rare occasion. The mailman delivered the mail as usual. I read the names on the envelopes and saw that one had my mother's name and the other was for the children of my father. I set in my mother's room in the dark rehearsing how I was going to talk to her about how I felt. It was night time when she came home and was startled by my presence. With tears in my eyes, I gave my mother the envelope with her name on it and said to her that it was for her. Then I showed her the other letter and said that it was for the children of my father and I needed things. I gave her the envelope and walked out of her room. *When I am grown I can live like I want, when I am grown I can live like I want.* I chanted to strengthen me and keep my faith strong.

I felt helpless as a child and spent many evenings under a parked car hiding from the handyman that had a key to our house. I would stay under the car until I saw my mother's car pass. I was scared of the handyman because he would lick his lips when I pass and stay say things a child should never hear let alone it being done to her. He was old, had grey hair, was chubby, and always reeked of alcohol and hamburger grease. I endured this for two years until I got the courage to speak up yet again. I told my mother that we needed to move or something bad was going to happen.

I was a good student, but I had issues. My hygiene wasn't the best. I didn't have enough clothes to cover a week of school so I would wear reruns in the same week. I would get laughed at and made fun of a lot.

One day at school, a classmate played a practical joke on me. I had place a chair behind me and when I sat, she had leaned the chair on it back legs and when I fell, the front legs poked me in the back. It was painful but I got up and slapped the shit out her and I was sent to the office. The principal called my home and Charles, one of my older brothers, came to the school. The principal explained his side of the story and I told mine. My brother believed me and told the principal that I did know where I was sitting because I had put the chair behind me. He went on to say that he didn't see the other little girl or her parents and that I had a right to slap the shit out of that little girl. The principal was speechless and I didn't get suspended.

Charles, My hero, I felt protected.

My mother came to me and said she had a surprise for me. She began jingling keys in my face and with excitement that we were moving. I felt love and valued for the first time. She packed me and my brothers into the car and went to see the house. It was a nice house, but it needed a lot of work. I didn't mind the work because it was a project that would involve the whole family. I worked as hard with my mother, pulling and whacking weeds, scrubbing the floors and washing walls. We finally moved in and I had my own room and it made me feel normal. One morning I woke up early and made me a bowl of cereal and begin watching cartoons. I was twelve and I loved watching School House Rock. I was singing along with Conjunction Junction when He exited my mother's room. He was tall, slim and handsome. He cared about how he looked, always taking pride in his appearance. He was the man that would later be called my daddy, my mother's teenage sweetheart. I first knew of him when I was I was about nine. We had moved from the Jordan Down Projects to South Central Los Angeles. (the house with the creepy handyman). I remember watching Soul Train and was bobbing my head to the music when he came in and without introduction, told me to get my feet off the coffee table. I looked up and told him, "You're not my daddy". He became angry and left. I went back to watching Soul Train with my arms tightly crossed while mumbling incoherent, rebellious things.

Henry was a married man. (Or was he in between marriages, I don't know.) He would show up now and then and I learn how to stay out of his way. I did see how happy my mother was when he was around, so I kept my distant not to aggravate him. My mother never had any other man for company and we were not required to call him uncle like so many of the neighborhood children would call the mother's boyfriends. I remembered that he would wear sandals and he had pretty feet. He was into black pride and had an air of a distinguished gentleman. I would watch him to see what he was about. I admired him for what I saw of him through a child's eye. I missed my dad, but I was glad to have a man around; a replacement or substitute. That substitute did not come without strings. Whenever he was not around, my mother would be withdrawn. Once my mother and I went to the grocery store and we were walking back home, a man offered us a ride and my mother accepted. He talked about taking me to Disneyland and I was excited because I had never been. As we pulled up to the house, my mother noticed that Henry was parked in the driveway. I wasn't so observant. As I got out of the car, I reminded the man about Disneyland. My mother took me in her room and beat me with a Deck shoe. I had tracks all over my legs and I laid on the floor trying to figure out what I had done. I learned to stay away from men.

I grew to be very angry, but when we moved to the new house, I felt that maybe this could be a new start.

Boy was I wrong.

After Henry was caught creeping out of her room, my mother decided that the house was not a good fit. We moved down the street to a duplex apartment. I thought that my mother and I would get one and my brothers would get the other one. Wrong yet again. My mother informed me that she needed her privacy and that I would have to live with my brothers in the other apartment. I was crushed and I felt rejected.

The substitute was now taking my mother away and I started becoming withdrawn myself. I had no one to talk to and I felt that my brothers weren't around. We didn't have a mother. Yes she paid the bills for us to have a roof over our head but that was where it ended. We were back to where the only meal we would have was dinner. I would look in the refrigerator and see evaporated milk and a piece of onion. I survived by chanting "When I'm grown I can live like I want".

I had to shut down my feeling, because I felt unwanted and my self-esteem was becoming nonexistent. I did poorly in school and never wanted bring attention to myself. I latched on to the first person who paid me attention.

My childhood sweetheart.

Chapter 4

Junior was smart and proper. He didn't talk like the neighborhood kids and I liked that. He made me feel special and I felt that we could be happy together.

Junior and I never went out on dates because we were too young for one and we lived next door to one another. We played basketball and other games, he was my friend. I admired him and thought that God had sent someone to love me. He made living in the apartment with my brother's and being rejected by my mother feel less hurtful. He would show me how to do things, like use better grammar. I started taking better care of myself; fixing my hair, reading more and doing better in school. I wanted a better life because the one I had was without basic needs. I was just surviving and not living.

Junior was a boy, and boys were taught by men, friends and parents. I knew he had his own issues and I thought that we would take care of one another. He provided for me and I would give him love that he was not getting at home. He was in an abusive household. He lived with his parents arguing and fighting each other. I had never heard an adult cuss at children let alone beat them with wooden boards. I felt sorry for him and I was willing to save him because he was saving me. I was in love.

Junior wanted to explore my body and with a 36 C at the age of twelve and his upbringing, it was the beginning of first base. Touching and feeling me up then maybe a little look see. I would only go so far because I was not comfortable with the sex thing. I was only fourteen and had not been talked to about sex, so I didn't know what to make of this feelings. The butterflies in my groin area felt funny and I was too young to have sex. I wanted to wait until marriage and I felt that we were going too fast. I tried talking him out of it but he would only ignore me if I didn't let him have his way.

Thank God he was still on the feeling me up stage and not intercourse. I uncomfortably allowed him to explore my body because I didn't want him to ignore me as before. I told myself that all boys do this and that I was still a virgin. It was important for me to married as a virgin. I wanted to be different than girls in the hood and I felt different. I felt that I was born in the wrong era and that I had to make the best out of the situation. Later in life I realized that I was pimping myself at the age of fourteen.

Junior's family moved more than fifty miles away and I lost my friend. I became withdrawn again and felt that I lost the only one who loved me. I started doing poorly in school and didn't know how I was going to escape this life that I hated. I would not talk to any other boys because I was in love with Junior and wanted him to come back for me. My high school years were a blur. I remember when I was in tenth grade. One evening, I was home alone and Junior came by. I hadn't heard from him in a while and I figured he had forgotten about me. I was so happy to see him but not that happy. He wanted to have sex and I was not going to do that. I did the usual touchy feely thing and let him play with my now 38 D's but I guarding my

cookie like the Hope diamond. On one of his visits, he got angry with me because he was not going to take no for an answer. I told him I couldn't do it and he drove me home all erratic and wouldn't look at me when I said bye. He sped off and that was the end of that. I mourned the lost yet again of this smart guy who was about to graduate with honors. He was also the only black guy that I knew was in the boys scouts. I thought he was my Prince Charming and I had lost him. In my despair, I went to Melanie, my older sister. I explained what had happen and that he broke up with me. I chose to take advice from a woman who had experience in the matter and because she was my big sister. She told me that we were in love and that it was alright to lose
my virginity to him because we were going to get married anyway so why wait. She told that I was going to be climbing the walls. I listened intently and was excited at the aspect of pleasing him.

The problem would be solved, I will have my love and I wouldn't feel alone anymore. The hope was restored and I hope that he would call me so I could tell him that I was ready. In my mind, Prince Charming was worth the Hope diamond and I was ready to give it to him gift wrapped. It was awhile before I would hear from him. I was getting more depressed by the days that went by.

Finally he came back after I don't know how long and I ran into his arms and told him I was ready. I jumped in his father's station wagon and we drove around for a while. We were too young to know about motels and decided to pull up in an abandon A&W root beer restaurant parking lot. I was scared but I didn't want to disappoint my

Prince Charming and make him angry. What lasted two minutes felt like an eternity. I felt pain and void of emotion. I tried to enjoy it because I was supposed to be climbing the walls but what I felt was my life going deeper in a pit. I resented him for making me feel that I had to do this and in the back of a station wagon in the back of abandon building.

I laid there for a few minutes as I covered by exposed body parts still waiting to be climbing the walls. What walls? I was in a station wagon and there were no walls. What have I done? I thought I was supposed to do this after I said I do. I was supposed to be on some island with a cool breeze blowing through the window. The sounds of waves advancing from the ocean, but I was in the back of a car feeling empty. I got myself together and sat up. I looked at Junior and asked if that was it? From the look on his face, I realized that I shouldn't have asked that. He looked embarrassed then he started to get angry. I began to explain that I thought I was supposed to be climbing the walls.

"What walls?" he said and I told him what my sister had said and he started laughing. I felt stupid but at least he didn't look angry anymore.

We got ourselves together and heading home. I felt like I has accomplished my goal of making him happy with me, until we reached my house and he said he had to hurry home. He didn't bother to turn off the engine. I got out of the car and he said he would see me later and as I closed the door he put the car in reverse and took off. I felt like I was garbage being dumped by the side of the road. I felt so hurt and transparent. I was afraid to go into the house because I felt so exposed. I finally got the courage to go into the house but I hid from everyone thinking that they would see what I had done. What had I done? I felt as though I gave away the Hope diamond and now I had nothing. A week had passed and I did not hear from Junior. I got anxious and my mind was going a million miles per second. I couldn't concentrate in school. I was scared and alone knowing that I had made a big mistake.

Chapter 5

I finally heard from Junior and he went on about living so far away and that he was breaking up with me because he was not able to see me because his father knew what we had done in his car and without transportation a long distance relationship was impossible. I was hurt, broken, and ashamed. I began to feel used and I felt that this was a lame excuse to discard me. I hung up the phone. What have I done? I know what I did. I gave away my Hope diamond not to Prince Charming but to a jerk. A horny toad and a few more choice name that I was to embarrass to say although I thought them.

Weeks went by and I thought a lot about what I had done and how foolish I had been. I was fifteen and I had given away my Hope diamond. I had nothing to offer my husband to be because I had given away the one thing the was precious. I thought about my sister and what she had said that Junior and I were going to get married anyway. She said we love each other and I didn't have to wait. I felt like such a fool and I was alone, withdrawn and ashamed.

My birthday was in a week and something didn't feel right. My breasts were tender and aunt flow had not made her visit. *Oh no, this can't be happening to me!* I would not…NO, I could not be pregnant. This would be the only gift that I got for my birthday and I didn't want it. I couldn't bring someone into a life I didn't want myself. I had no one to talk to about this. I was scared clueless and dumb as dirt. What did I know about pregnancy?!

I went back to my sister and told her what I

suspected. I told her that my breasts were tender and that my period was late. My sister jumped into action and made me an appointment for an exam with a doctor. I felt safe that help was on the way.

My sister went with me to the doctor. I barely remember it. I purposely blocked it out because a man that I didn't know was down there touching my now Cubic Zirconium.

The test results confirmed that I was pregnant. I told the doctor that I wanted my period and he had to do something to make it come. I did not know what that was but I wanted it done. I could not treat my own child the same way I was being treated. How selfish could I be? How would I support a child when I was a child myself?

"I don't do abortions," the doctor said snidely. "What did you think was going to happen?" He went on to say if I didn't want a child, I should have used birth control.

Birth control? What was that? I was so green, ignorant and I was still a child. I sat there being yelled at by a man that had just explored my cave and he was talking to me like this. I wanted to be helped, not ridiculed.

My sister, Melanie, sat there silently as if she had nothing to do with this, but I sat there taking this abuse.

Climbing the walls… yeah right.

We left the doctor's office. My sister turned to me and said, "Now you are just like us. You will have a baby out of wedlock." I envisioned knocking her off the curb into the street and a garbage truck running her over. What is birth control? I sat silently on the bus thinking about how I was going to tell my mother. I didn't want to tell my mother that. I wanted to be different and I certainly didn't want the life my sisters had. I wanted better and I wanted to be married before I had a family. Melanie went on and on but I didn't hear a word she said. I was in my own world of despair, confusion and lonely.

I went home and stayed to myself. While watching TV, I saw a commercial about unplanned pregnancy. I thought this was a Godsend. I wrote down the number and then called for an appointment.

I was in the tenth grade and I ditched school for the appointment. My head was hurting and I couldn't take it. The pain was like a nail being driven through my brain. I got to the clinic that was on Figueroa Street, downtown in Los Angeles.

It was crowded and busy. I went to the desk and I told her I had an unplanned pregnancy. I was given a clipboard and told to complete the forms. I had taken the medical card from my mother's drawer so I had the information needed. After I completed the forms and returned them to the receptionist, I set for what seem like hours. There were children there, babies crying and I began to cry because I didn't want that to be my child or me. My name was called and I followed the nurse into a room. She instructed me to disrobe and gave me a paper gown. 'The doctor would be in, in a minute," she said and left.

I did what she told me to do and I could still hear the children crying. Who would bring a child to a place like this? I looked at the walls and all the pictures of flowers on all the wall. The walls. I hate the walls. I didn't climb the walls.

The doctor entered the room with a nurse and told me what I already knew. I told him that I can't have a baby and I begin to get hysterical.

The nurse touched my hand and I became quiet. I put my hands to my face to hide it because I felt so ashamed. She told me that it would be alright as she handed me paper to sign.

I WANT TO TERMINATE THIS PREGANCY.

That was so big and bold and I checked the box. I was a child and I was making decision that would change my whole way of thinking. I was no longer a child anymore. I was at this clinic in a paper gown and I was scared.

The nurse came in and gave me a shot and instructed me that I was to lie down and the doctor will be in in ten minutes. Ten minutes, I laid there thinking about my life and the events that led up to this moment. I was alone in a room with flowers on the walls. I thought about Junior. I saw his face as he left me after giving him the Hope diamond. I thought about the lame excuse he gave me for the break up. I thought about my mother. I didn't want to disappoint my mother. As I laid there I felt a tear roll across my cheek into my ears.

The ten minutes were over and the doctor and nurse entered the room. A machine was turned on and I heard a humming noise and my body tensed up.

"Relax," the doctor said, as the nurse held my hand.

I went to a special place in my mind that was peaceful and I heard nothing. I then felt something being inserted into my body and I began to leave my special place. I was fully conscious and I was terrified. I felt a back and forth motion and it was awful. Then I heard a sucking noise and I turned to see a container and it was being filled with blood. I wanted to pass out but I needed to see what was happening. I wish I had my mother. Wait, no. I wouldn't want my mother to see me like this. I was alone, so I went back to the special place in my mind where I heard nothing, I saw nothing and I felt nothing.

The procedure was over and the doctor inserted a tampon into my vaginal. I felt degraded and devalued. I wanted to say something but I felt I had no right. I was in a clinic. I got what I wanted. I got my period back.

I was given instructions not to have sex for six weeks and to take the antibiotics that I was given. I did what I was told.

I went to my sister and made her promise never to tell that I was pregnant. I told her that I terminated that pregnancy and she seemed disappointed. I explained that I was too young and that I couldn't take care of a child. I was in tenth grade, I had not work experience and the boyfriend that was in love with me and that I was going to married had broken up with me after accepting my Hope diamond that I had given up willingly. My sister promised to keep it to herself and I went on my way.

Chapter 6

Months later, I got a call from Junior and I was both numb and excited. He talked about how much he missed me and that he had use of another car. I thought my Prince Charming was back and my life was back on track. I told him that I loved him and that my life was uneventful because he wasn't in it.

I was now in the eleventh grade and during poorly in school, while Junior was graduating with honors. He earned an Eagle Scout badge and I was proud of him. He asked if I could be at the ceremony and I was honored, but my mother said I couldn't go even though he was coming to get me. I threw a tantrum. I was yelling and crying because I felt that my mother was standing in the way of my future. He wanted me and I wanted him. After much persuasion my mother gave in and I wanted to surprise him so I caught the bus to his house which was more than fifty miles away.

When I got to his house he was surprise to see me and boy was he surprised. I was in the bathroom getting dressed and I heard someone talking in the living room. The voice wasn't familiar but I figured it was a relative that was also going to the ceremony. As I came out of the bathroom Junior met me in the hallway and took me into his room. His parents were okay with it and I didn't mind because I loved him. I thought we were going to make out but he began to explain about the voice that I had heard in the living room. It was his date.

His date!

I thought I was his girl. What is he talking

about? I felt betrayed and embarrassed. How was I going to come out of the room without feeling like I had egg on my face? I thought of my mother and how she was saying that it was not a good idea for me to come here but here I was. I sat there on Junior's bed thinking of what I could do. *Do what you do best Marilyn and guard your heart.* I walked out of the room and greeted everyone in the room even his date. I was a friend of the family and that was that. Junior's sister sat with me and talked about his date but I said nothing bad about her. In my mind I cursed Junior in every way imaginable. How could he have a date? I was his girlfriend and I didn't date. What was he thinking? He was supposed to love me and he had a date.

We got to the ceremony and I sat there with a broken heart then I heard them call his name. I felt proud of him in spite of what he had done. Junior always spoke of the Eagle badge and the honor behind it. For a black man to get an Eagle badge was an honor indeed. I quickly forgot about the pain and embarrassment I felt and was glad I came even though the surprise was on me.

After the ceremony his girlfriend/date started looking at me like she knew I was not just a family friend and I didn't care. She looked me up and down as if that was going to intimidate me. She didn't know me. I have mastered pain and embarrassment and I knew how to keep a cool head. I would not let the likes of her make me show my pain and hurt I felt in my heart. The date was gone and it was time to take care of business. I took Junior in the garage and told him that I wasn't mad at him. He made a choice and he said that he thought I wasn't coming because of what my mother had said. As he continued to explain I stopped listening because I knew he was lying anyway. I seduced him in the backseat of his father's station wagon and then told him that the badge he earned was not earned at all. He didn't have integrity, there was no honor and he was not trustworthy. I told him that we were through and the conversation was over.

I slept in his sister's room and thought of my decision and knew it was best for me. There was guilt that I seduced him but I had to get my power back. After much rationalization, I drifted off to sleep. I went back home the next morning and never spoke of my trauma. It was embarrassing and I was ashamed.

I went back to school and I acted like my usual self. Strong, in charge, and lonely. I did minimal in school, only what I needed to pass the class. I often thought about how I felt and it wasn't a good feeling. I often felt ugly and unwanted. My life was void of love and care and I had a lot of love in my heart. I was friendless, but I talked to people. I would listen to what they were going through and thought if they only knew my pain they would think they had it good and they didn't have trouble at all.

I had no idea that, that moment back of the station wagon, in that garage was going to come back to bite me in my butt. It couldn't be. I was on birth control pills and I only missed one but I took it as soon as I remembered. My breasts were tender and my head was hurting. I remember this feeling and I didn't like it. I thought about my period and I was at least a week late.

Another ditch day to the clinic and I was alone, an all too familiar feeling. I was sixteen and back again. Those damned walls was all I could think

about because it kept me from facing the truth. I was here solving the problem from a bad choice that I had made. I wasn't raised like this, but then I felt that I wasn't raised at all. My home life was life and I didn't have anyone to talk to and I dare not tell my sister. Climbing the walls, I starting to laugh to keep from crying but the reality was that I was back at the clinic.

I knew what to expect this time and it was easier. I checked the familiar box that I wanted to terminate the pregnancy and it didn't seem so big and so bold this time. There were still children in the office and I saw that family planning was not working. Babies crying and again, I thought that can't be me. The rationalization starting in my head and I said to myself it is what it is, get over it. I thought of my decision to end the relationship with Junior and this time it was all me. I was sixteen sitting in a clinic waiting to end a pregnancy and I was strong. I didn't needing my mother. I didn't need anyone but the doctor who was going to fix this.

After the procedure was completed, I told the doctor that I would insert the tampon myself and he looked at me as if I was a pro. At that point, he knew that I was not a newbie.

I left the clinic feeling like the deed was done and I could get on with my life. I notice a plane flying high in the sky. I thought about joining the military and starting a career in the Air force. I was fearless and I wanted to fly planes. It was time to think about my future.

As I sat at the bus stop with the antibiotic

and I started to think about my life and what I wanted. To get out of the life that was given to me. Not to die, but to fight for what was rightfully mine. To get out of poverty and to live like I wanted to live. Without lacking any needs, to be independent and not needing anyone. I knew of God, and I believed that he loved me but I wanted to feel his hugs. The hug of a parent, an older sister, or brother. To feel that someone cared about me and yet I sat at this bus stop alone.

I went back to school the next day as if nothing had happened. I dared not tell anyone, not even the one person that I called friend. I would look at my peers in class and think of how lucky they were. The clothes that they wore, the activities they were involved in, and how they participated in class. I hid so no one would notice the clothes I wore today I wore on Monday.

I felt that my life sucked and I was trying to figure out what I could do for a better life. I went to speak to a counselor who didn't hear a word I said. She took one look at my grades and figured I was a lost cause. I was convinced to pick up a trade of cosmetology because I told her I like doing hair. I told her I wanted to go into the military and that I wanted to be a pilot. I needed someone to see me, but I was still invisible.

I did what I was told and started going to another school part time while still attending my high school. That was not without its problems. I had to catch a school bus to the other school and my gym teacher didn't like me because I was honest and I told her what was on my mind. I was treated unjustly and she wouldn't let me leave and I would often miss my bus.

She knew what she was doing and I told her so. She threatened to slap me and I told her she will get slapped back. I was not backing down. She was standing in my way of progress to get out of the ghetto and I was mad. I told her that she should be ashamed of herself and asked what did I do to her for her to be so mean?. I noticed that she had a bruise on her face and I told her to leave him or stay, but I will not let her take her frustrations out on me. With a surprised look, she then opened the gate, but I missed my bus anyway.

I went to school and came home and I would go hit tennis balls on the side of a vacant building. That was my life.

Chapter 7

One Friday night, Junior dropped by and asked me to take him back. He told me that he loved me and that he was sorry about what happen at the ceremony. I was hard and I look at him like he was crazy. He started to cry and I could feel his pain, my pain and I just hugged him trying to make the pain go away from the both of us. I started to cry and I told him I had to tell him something. I told him of the abortions and how alone I felt. I told him that we weren't together and I didn't want him to think I was trying to trap him. He held me until I stopped crying and told me that he understood why I did what I did and I got my hug. It felt good to confess what I had done because I never spoke to anyone about it. The weight was lifted and I felt loved again.

It was Christmas, and Junior came to see me. He bought me this beautiful necklace of a gold arrow pointing downward. To me it was priceless and the meaning had important significance. He explained that he understood all my decisions, but that if I got pregnant again that I promised to not abort his child and I promised.

I was happy and I was in love and I felt that Junior loved me. He took care of me. He was working and didn't mind providing my needs. He bought all my necessities and then some. I had never been made to feel like I mattered.

My family would make comments about Junior, but he was the one treating me with love and kindness. I was so enamored with the attention. I went around the apartment humming songs like

Endless love and Ain't No Stopping Us Now. Junior was ready to settle down and I would be graduating in June, a week before my eighteenth birthday. Although I was using birth control my breast were tender and I began to worry. Even though the relationship was going well I didn't want to start a family before married and before we were settled. I didn't want to ignore the feelings that were all too familiar.

Ditch day yet again but I needed to know. On the bus I went to the fix it clinic, but this time it was only to confirm the pregnancy. The necklace gave me the security I needed.

Keeping the promise that I made on Christmas day would be easy. By this time I knew the routine, except this time I checked that I wanted to get prenatal information. I was examined and then the nurse was about to give me the shot; the one I knew all too well. I asked her what the shot was for and she said for the procedure. I asked what procedure and she looked at me like I knew good and well what procedure she was talking about. I told her that I was keeping the baby and the if that shot was supposed to get me ready for the "procedure" she needed to look at my chart. The nurse quickly left the room and I got up to get dressed all the while thinking about what was about to happen. There was a knock on the door and I answered giving permission to enter. The doctor asked me if I was alright and I was more concerned about the nurse. I told the doctor to tell her that I was alright and I thanked him for the service. I then asked for a copy of verification of the pregnancy because I was afraid to tell my mother in my own voice. I would rather that she read the information.

I caught the bus home and thought about my future. The military was out of the question because I would never leave my child for someone else to raise and in my family and in Junior's, there wasn't any picking. They didn't have a nurturing bone in their body. From the bus, I saw a plane.

"Bye plane." I said. I missed my chance.

When I got home, my mother was giving Henry the care that was meant for me but I didn't care anymore. I had Junior and now we were going to be a family. I rubbed the downward arrow and gave her the paper. She read it and said "Ah Marilyn". Henry took the paper and said "She is about to graduate. It will be alright." The look on my mother's face spoke volumes. I walked away feeling that I let her down, but what was done was done. I waited for Junior to call me and I told him that I needed to see him.

I went to school and was informed that my grades were not good and that if I didn't pass I was not going to graduate. I made a commitment to myself and my child that I will graduate. I started participating and asking for extra credit work to bring my grade up.

Junior came down from Pomona and I told him that we were going to have a baby. I asked him if he really meant what he said when he gave me the necklace because this is a big responsibility and if he couldn't handle it I needed to know now. As he gazed in my eyes, he told me that he meant every word. We were now a family and that was scary and exciting at the same time.

I was still in school and decided to stay with my mother until I graduated. I studied hard so that I was able to walk across the stage.

Dealing with morning sickness was no joke. I was queasy and tired, but I continued with my studies so that I wouldn't be dead weight to Junior. My brothers were not happy with me. They would say things about my condition and that they thought I was better than that. Better than what? Out of nine siblings, I was the second to graduate and I'm number eight of the nine. My expectations didn't change, only my circumstances. I wasn't proud of how I did things but I was not going to take being belittled and say nothing. I wanted out of this life of poverty and dysfunction and I wasn't going to let anyone make me feel bad about it

I got my final grades and earned four A's and a B. My brother and his wife went to my graduation, but my mother was a no show. I was three months pregnant but I graduated and I was happy. I considered myself an adult and the life that I felt I deserved was about to begin.

I moved to Pomona with Junior who had his own place that he shared with a roommate. He was a hard worker and I admired his confidence. He was tidy and living with him was great. I loved the order that he had in his life. I was three months pregnant and unemployed, but I considered myself as a soon to be housewife. I depended solely on Junior for my basic needs. I had never been treated with such care and love, and I wanted to please him. Sex was great and I was now enjoying our time together. I felt that he loved me for me and not because he was trying to get anything from me but love in return. Dinner was always ready when he got home and we would make midnight runs to the market when I had crazy cravings.

Chapter 8

When I was seven months pregnant and his roommate was out of town, Junior shocked the hell of me. That was the day my fairy tale story became a nightmare. He came home and was very angry. He was snapping at me and was very short with me. I told him that I didn't deserve the treatment that I was receiving and that he must want to be alone. When I went to get up from the sofa he came to me and started slapping me in my face. I was in shock because I had never been beaten like this. I realized, I went from no attention to being beat like a punching bag. I was terrified and my only thought was of the safety of my unborn child. I did not fight back because I didn't was to make it worse. I thought, what could have caused this? I tried to recall what I had said to get this kind of reaction, but nothing I said should have ever cause him to hit me. I ended up on the floor with him standing over me saying so now you are going to leave me but you can't have an abortion and walked out. Leaving me dazed and in pain and in shock, I cried not knowing what to do. I was not working I had no money or transportation. I called my mother and I couldn't speak. She kept saying hello and finally I was able to say mom. I repeated " Mom, mom, mom," then she said my name. "Marilyn, what's wrong?" I told her that he hit me mom. My mother said once a man hit you he will never stop. I told her that I would be alright and I hung up the phone. I didn't want to believe that. I was seven months pregnant and he was my Prince Charming. This was a nightmare I wanted to wake up from. Right now! No right now. This was not the plan. I had given him the love that he had never got in his family and he, until this, had given me the love I needed. It wasn't material things, or too much attention. I didn't take up all his time. He went to Karate practice and he didn't have to worry about things at home. I was totally loyal to him and he beat me like a dog.

After the shock wore off the angry set in. How dare he hit me? I was grown. He couldn't re-raise me. My daddy died when I was eight and even then my daddy never hit me. I got up off the floor and went to take a shower while the beating replayed in my head.

After my shower, I eased into bed and laid there thinking of what I have got myself into. I didn't come from a family of domestic violence. My mother didn't even use profanity. She didn't listen to secular music nor did she drink.

He was always gentle with me. Okay, he cheated on me, and he deserted me when I needed him most, but I thought that was immaturity. I thought he had out grown that stuff. Got darned! He earned an Eagle scout badge, and that had to mean something. I was trying to understand why I wished he was here to comfort me and I thought, What's wrong with this picture. That man just beat you like a dog. What do I do now? I was alone, scared and becoming a victim. I stopped crying of thought of my next move. I couldn't be in this situation. It was not healthy for me or my unborn child.

The next morning when I woke, I was stiff and bruised. I was afraid to move but I forced myself to get up. I came out of the bedroom to go brush my teeth and was greeted by remorse, regret and tears. Junior had made breakfast and waited anxiously to serve me. I didn't want to look at him because I had the results of last night's altercation all over my face. My lip was swollen, I had a knot on my forehead and a bruise on the side of my face. He grabbed me and held me as he cried and I could feel my body tense up. This was the man that savagely beat a woman who was seven months with his child. He felt my tension and started pleading for me not to leave him. He had a fear on his face that I couldn't describe. A look of desperation and fear that he looked more wounded than I felt if that could be possible. I began to feel sorry for him and I began to cry.

I saw standing before me the little boy that was physically abused as a child. I remembered the day I first saw him. I was hanging clothes on the line, when I heard this crack and then a child crying. As I looked up, I saw this tall thin woman with nine kids trailing behind her from oldest to youngest like ducks. The oldest was Junior and he was crying and holding his head. I was thirteen and he was fifteen. I wanted to give him a hug, I felt his pain. The woman leading the pack was carrying a board and I assumed that that was her rod for which she kept her brood in line.

I had never known of anyone being hit with a board. I've had spankings with switches and even an extension cord but never a stick. Tears welled into my eye for this boy who cried in pain.

The man that cried before me was the child I saw back then and I wanted to comfort him. I wanted to make the pain go away, both mine and his. I hugged him and told him that everything was going to be alright. I prayed silently while I held him for God to bring peace to this unsettled home. The home that I made for myself was filled with misery and pain.

We got ourselves together and he sat me down at the table. I remember the spread on the table. Bacon, eggs, grits, toast and orange juice was before me and I had no appetite to eat it but I eat with enthusiasm for his benefit. He needed to feel accepted and I needed my man back.

After breakfast was over, the beating was never spoken of again. We went on as if nothing happened. I felt that I didn't have a life; I just existed.

We would go visit our family. His mother would talk about us being married before the baby came. I would make up an excuse of why we would wait and she stated that if we were not married then my baby would be a demon. My maternal instinct took over and I told her that she will not talk about my baby like that. She had no right to call my baby a demon when her son had issues that I know she had to know about.

I was ready to go, but Junior was not ready to leave and I just sat there quietly. The thoughts of this alcoholic, filthy mouth woman calling my baby a demon enraged me. I would never treat my child as I had witnessed her treating hers.

The treatment was no different from my family. They would talk about me behind my back. The joke was on me. I thought I had it so good and I was just another statistic of domestic violence among other dysfunctions. Junior would always make sure I looked my best in front of my family and he didn't mind me being alone with them because he knew that I would not go whining to them about my situation. He knew that he had me where he wanted me.

Alone.

The better I looked the angrier my siblings got and my mother would pray for me to stop from worrying about me. She always defended me and that only made the rivalry that more intense.

Everything was back to normal and I thought that Junior had gotten the episode out of his system until a conversation had occurred about my brothers. He talked about the drug use and how he was uncomfortable when he was around them. I told him that the next time I visit he could just drop me off. He looked at me as to say *oh, no she didn't* and I look at him to say *oh, yes I did.* He tried to intimidate me but I was not going to go through life being afraid to speak what was on my mind.

One night, he was entertaining some friends of his and because they were all men, I made sure he had everything that he needed and made myself scarce. While I was in the room, I could smell marijuana wafting through the door. I went to the bathroom and watched him as he enjoyed himself. I couldn't believe it. He felt uncomfortable around my brothers while he sat in the living room with these white boys hitting a bong. The fool probably didn't know how to roll a joint. I shook my head in disbelief and went back in the room.

After his dude fest was over, he tried to come in the bedroom and hump me like I was the munchies. I was now eight months pregnant and tired not to mention sick of his phoniness. I try to pretend I was sleep and he tried to have sex with me anyway. What is wrong with this fool? This is sick and pathetic. I felt him trying to pull my underwear down and the Ike and Tina drama begin.

When I protested he began to try and take what I was not in the mood to give. I saw my Grandfather and my brother in law. They didn't get it and neither was Junior. He will have to kill me now but I won't be a victim, not for anyone. I kicked him until he got off of me and then I told him I was leaving. That was something that I refused to let happen. He left the room as I started packing a bag and getting dressed at the same time.

As I headed for the door, he met me in the door way. I turn around because it reminded me of my grandfather standing in the doorway looking at me like I was lunch. I got my composure, then turned to face him. I told him to get out of my way and he just stood there. When I tried to get pass him, he grabbed me and threw me on the bed. I jumped up and just looked at him. He then grabbed a chair from the corner of the room and sat it in the middle of the floor. He pushed me back down on the bed and told me that was I was not going anywhere as he sat in the chair and produced a knife.

This was no steak knife, but a butcher knife. I could do nothing but look at him. I began to assess the degree of danger and thought this is it. He was breathing hard and began telling me that he could kill me. I was scared to death and the life I wanted looked as though I would never get to see it. I remained calm and refused to show fear. I looked at the knife, then at Junior. I looked passed him to the door and then to the window behind me. I was on the second floor and eight months pregnant, there was no way I could get away. I looked at Junior again and started to laugh. I kept laughing and he looked at me bewildered. I laughed so hard that he started to laugh. He dropped the knife and came to hug me but I kept on laughing. The weight of him cause us to both fall back on the bed. He laughed and asked me why I was laughing and I told him after looking at the door and the window, I figured that I was screwed but I refused to beg for my life. I could not give him the satisfaction of seeing fear in me. He told me I was crazy and I agreed.

Lying in the arms of a psycho, crazy.

That fool still tried to have sex but I couldn't stomach that like I ate the breakfast. I told him that I was exhausted and needed to go to sleep.

After hours of lying in his arms, I finally fell to sleep.

Chapter 9

The next morning was not expected. Oh, I thought that I was going to wake up, because I knew he didn't have the balls to kill me. He was a scared little boy who was screaming for attention and I alone was his audience. I got up to use the bathroom with an eight month old belly. Junior was still asleep or was he pretending. I didn't care. My Prince was turning more and more into a toad.

I begin to brush my teeth and found out that I could not spit. I looked at my face in the mirror, but didn't see anything wrong. I tried to spit again and I got scared and tears welled into my eyes. A tear fell from my right eye, but the left kept filling with tears. I tried to blink but couldn't, but only my right eye would close. My tears became vocal as Junior heard my cry. He came to the bathroom but I refused to let him in.

I was deformed.

The left side of my face was not moving. I still had feeling in my face but the left side was not moving.

What was wrong?

I thought I had a stroke.

Junior was pounding on the door and I finally let him in. I was still crying with my hands in my face and I told him that my face was broken. He snatched my hand down and the look on his face made me cry more. I was ugly, fat and now deformed.

I tried to control my emotions but that only made me look worse. What was I going to do now? I had no intentions of staying with this abusive man and I looked like a monster. I told Junior, I wanted to go home to my mother and he tried to talk me out of leaving, but I convinced him to take me home.

When my mother saw my face, she was also scared. She didn't know what to say and I didn't want to hear anything. I figured that with all of the emotional and physical abuse that I had received from Junior that my face had just quit working.

I went to the doctor and was told that I had Bells Palsy. The thoughts in my head were for him to fix it. He had a name and seemed familiar with this condition. The doctor explained that because I was pregnant that I couldn't have the treatment because it involved shock therapy and drugs that would be harmful to the child.

I left the doctor's office feeling discouraged and hopeless. Here I was eighteen, eight months pregnant by a nigga who beats the shit out of me. I had no education other than high school and I was fat even without a baby in my stomach. I had no work experience and now I was deformed because my face was paralyzed by something call Bells Palsy.

I thought about Junior and felt that I had no choice but to stick it out with him and pray to God that things would change. I never told him that I had intention to leave and never look back. Looking back, the face that I would have not been looking back with was now paralyzed. I had emotions and all my pain on one side and a blank stare of the other. I was a mess. I was trapped.

I went back to my mother's house to figure out a plan of my next move. I made a check list.

Go and apply for Welfare,

Figure how to keep Junior calm so he won't have a reason the whoop my ass

Not get on my mother's nerves for her to kick me out

Save my money

Find a Job

I went to my mother and explained my intentions. "I want to come back home." The look on her face was, no way. I told her about applying for Welfare and that I would start paying her rent. She was fine with that.

Check, I had found what drove her decision to allow me to stay.

Money!

The next morning I went to the Welfare office by myself and sat for hours, me and big stomach. How did I get here I thought, Oh, listening to my dumb ass sister telling me I was going to be climbing the walls. Giving away the Hope Diamond to a nigga I thought was my Prince. Not to mention my low self-esteem I got from many year of being told that I was ugly, and stupid resulting in me feeling invisible. I realized that I put myself there me and me alone. My family, the school system, and my poverty was not an excuse. I had chanted for years about living the way I wanted when I was grown and I was getting off to a bad start.

As I set in the Welfare office I looked around at the people and thought this is not my life, but it was. I had reduced myself to a statistic of teen pregnancy, unwed mother, and black uneducated female.

My name was called and I went to the

worker who was going to hear my sob story. I sat down and waited for a command. She looked over my paper work and then looked at me.

Another one bites the dust, I feel like I was disappearing as I sat there. She asked why I was applying for AFDC, which is cash aid, food stamps and medical. I looked down at my stomach then I looked back at her. I thought to myself, oh she is going to make me tell how foolish I was.

I began by telling the worker that I thought I was going to get married but Junior started beating me and that I had to leave for the safety of myself and that of my child. I spoke from the language of TV. To others it was a baby, my little girl, but to me it was my child.

It became a déjà vu of the doctor's office. Didn't you know about getting pregnant and why are you doing it? I was too ashamed to admit that I was taking birth control but I was too immature to remember to take them on time so I said nothing.

The interview ended and I was dismissed with the knowledge to know that my eligibility would be determined in about thirty days and I would receive a letter in the mail.

I went back home and told my mother what happened and promise that when I got my first check I would give her the money. I tried hard to appease her because I didn't want her to be angry and kick me out. She had the power in her hands. I didn't blame her, she didn't tell me to do what I did. She was a woman that was left with seven children in a home to raise alone. She didn't ask for five of them to still be in her house, grown and acting let baby birds still looking for her to feed them.

I received a letter from the District

Attorney's office with an appointment for child support. I called Junior to get the information needed for the appointment. We were still talking and he gave it to me.

The day of the appointment, I was nervous and didn't know what to expect. As I sat there waiting I thought, what kind of attitude I was going to have to face? My name was called and I did what was instructed. I sat down facing a stoned face woman behind the desk, who gave me a questionnaire to complete. I couldn't believe the questions.

Where did I have sex?

How many times I had sex?

How many partners did I have?

Who else knew about the relationship?.

Even describe his dick. Size. Scars. Etc. oh come on!

After I complete the form, the worker verbally asked me the same questions. I told her that the information was on the form and I refused to repeat it. I didn't want to hear myself repeat it. I had his social security number, Driver's license number and address. What more did she want? I told her to ask him but I was not going to be mistreated and tortured or belittled. She asked another question and I stopped listening. I repeated the answer was on the form that I had completed. I could have jumped over that table and beat the shit out of the lady but I needed the money.

I was dismissed again with the warning that if they couldn't reach him it could hinder me getting my aid. Fuck you, bitch. I thought with a smile.

I went back to my mother's house and

waited and waited and waited. I cleaned the house and cooked the dinners. I also wondered where my life was going to end up. I had a strong will to get out of the mess, but I didn't have a clue of what to do.

I heard the mail man putting mail in the slot and I rushed out to ask him how to get a job working for the post office. He happened to have an application on him and gave it to me. I was excited; I felt that God was looking down on me even though I messed up. I completed that application and put it up for the next day.

My brother, Charles and I got into an argument about I don't know what and he mentioned that I thought that I was a Miss Goody two shoes but that he knew I had an abortion and I wasn't perfect after all. I was speechless and all I could think about is that Melanie promised.

Later, Jeff, and Jerry on two separate occasions stated that they knew that I had had an abortion. I realized that the secret was that I didn't know that everybody knew. Melanie had told everyone. I wondered if my mother knew and I began to worry. I didn't want my mother to know unless it came from me. I had to tell her myself and soon because it was only a matter of time before loose lips were going to sink my ship.

I got the nerve to tell my mother. We were alone in the house and I asked her to sit down because I had something to tell her. I began the story and I told the truth. I first asked her if anybody told her that I had an abortion and she said no. I then told her that I did, but I went even further. I told her that I had had two abortions. Her face had no emotion and I could not read it. I explained that I felt that I didn't have any options and that I could not care for a baby by myself. I told her that I felt bad but that I will take care of the baby that I now carried. My mother eased my shamed by telling me she understood without judgment. I was freed from the blackmail threats of my siblings and I felt liberated.

Chapter 10

Junior had been calling and my heart was getting soft. I did miss him and he seemed so sorry and he said he love me and would never hit me again. My mother's voice came to me. *Once a man hit you he will do it again.* I wasn't hearing that. I was in a bad predicament. Who was going to want a deformed, fat, unemployed woman with a baby and I wanted my child to be raised with both parents?

I caved in.

I moved back with Junior but I still paid my mother rent. My address remained in Los Angeles, but I was trying to make my relationship work in Pomona.

I walked on pins and needles for a month in a half. Junior was on his best behavior, but he acted like a sex addict. There was no rest for the weary and I dared not say no. I enjoyed being with him and I thought I liked sex. In the meantime, I would make candy apples and eat all I wanted before giving the rest to the neighborhood children.

I craved candy apples.

The due date of December 2nd, had come and went and my labor started on the eleventh. My dumb ass sister had moved to the same apartment building we were living in and she was expecting a baby too. At six o'clock in the morning the pain hit me. It felt like a bad back ache. I didn't know what it was and I didn't want to complain. I made Junior lunch and kissed him goodbye then I got dressed and called my sister. I loved her and I wanted her to love me back but felt that she was intentionally putting obstacles in my life and I didn't know why.

My sister told me to come down to her apartment and I did. The contractions were getting strong now and it was getting harder to bare. My sister said I should go to the hospital, but I didn't want to go alone and without Junior.

Junior arrived and took me to the hospital. He was driving slow and I thought he really cared about me. Ooh he does love me and I really loved him too. There were no episodes since I came back and I was relieved.

We arrived at the hospital and went right to Labor and Delivery. Junior was concerned and attentive. I needed that from him and I knew that I was going to be alright. The pains were intense, but I was brave. I rode the pain and felt that with every contraction I was becoming a woman, a soon to be mother. I had my mind on being a good mother, someone who will be there for my child , to provide for her and give her protection in life. It was no longer about me, but my child who didn‘t ask for this life. I begin to talk to Junior between a contraction, while I was distracted by someone screaming in the hall way. I started to get scared, because I began thinking that I will have to go through what they were going through. I heard my name and when I looked up; my sister was standing in the doorway with a red face and tears streaming down her face. I had been calm until that moment, but I started cry and getting hysterical. I began to get scared and my cool demeanor went out the window. I started to chant that she will be alright to calm myself down. My sister had had three children before this and if she was acting like this, I had hell to look forward to and this was just the calm before the storm.

The nurse came into the room to calm me down, but all I could hear were my sister's blood curdling screams. I asked the nurse to go and check on her because I was worried about her and she was eight year older than me.

The nurse came back and told me that my sister had her baby, but she was still screaming. I yelled for her to shut the hell up. I became angry that she would make such a scene. She was supposed to be a role model or an example for her younger sister but it made me terrified.

I can do this, I can do this but I will not make a fool of myself. I was a woman and I refused to act like a nigga and make a spectacle of myself. I got myself into this and I was going to come out of it alright.

I was in labor for over twenty hours and the nurse was trying to encourage me saying that she could see her but I knew she was lying because it felt and looked like the baby was sitting in my chest.

The doctor came in to examine me and that was painful. I tried to contain myself, but I couldn't hold back the screams. My face and the Bells Palsy made me look like I was in a circus mirror. You know the one that made you look contorted but I didn't care, it was in pain. He got the forceps and I thought about them injuring my child. I begged him not to use the forceps. My body started to shake and my doctor decided it was time to do a cesarean section.

A form was thrown in my face and I signed it. I just wanted this over. I could barely sign my name I was so weak. They prepped me for surgery and then I was out.

When I awoke, I saw two babies and I asked if I had twins, but it was the drugs.

I passed out.

I woke up a day later and asked to see my baby, but the nurse said that I had a fever and was not able to see the baby yet. I needed two units of blood and I was very weak . I yearned to see my baby, but I would patiently wait because I wanted what was best for my daughter. It was a girl and I just thought of all the love that I had for the child that I had not yet seen.

Junior came to see me and he was wearing a hospital gown. I asked him why and he told me he had just got through feeding our daughter. I felt robbed, but at least he was able to bond with our child.

The nurse came into the room and said that I was a good patient and it was hard to believe that that other lady was my sister. She said she complained too much. It was always something but I had gone through so much and didn't complain at all. I thought to myself, I was successful in not being a nigga. The nurse went on to talk about my daughter that she was beautiful and that made me want to see her all the more. It would be three days before I laid eyes on her and she was beautiful. She was dark like a Hershey Kiss, plump like a teddy bear and had a head full of jet black hair.

She was prefect.

It was time to go home after five days and I and looked forward to be getting on with my new life. I had five days to figure out what kind of mother I was going to be. A mother that I never had. I would give lots and hugs and kisses, make sure she had everything that she needed, I would encourage her at all time, but must of all I would be honest and put her first. She became my strength and my reason to live an abundant life.

Junior and I decided to name her Candace. A name I found in the Bible. A warrior that brought someone through a great war. Yes, Candace was a warrior.

We arrived home and I was tired. My stomach hurt from all the stitches. I walked upstairs and put Candace in the crib that her daddy had purchased and built while we were in the hospital. He had put a card in it that said Welcome Home, Candace. I laughed because it was so cute but I decided to wait till later to offer correction. I was in the moment and I knew that Junior didn't like being criticized, so way ruin it.

I rested for a week and then I begged Junior to take me to see my mother. Junior did what I had asked. I got dressed and when I was about to walk down the stairs I saw myself falling with Candace in tow. I put Candace down, dropped the diaper bag, took off my Candies and walked Candace down the stairs barefoot. What I had seen was trippy, but I didn't want it to happen so I took precautions.

My family was there to see the baby and they commented on the way I looked with my Candies shoes, my silk blouse and my polyester pants. Yes I said polyester. Around my neck was the necklace that caused Candace to be. I was proud of my family. Yes, Junior, Candace and I were a family. I felt that my life was complete, so all the stares, the nasty comments and the attitude in the air did not faze me.

I felt complete.

Chapter 11

Candace was a month old and all hell broke loose. I was down stairs sitting on the floor watching my baby coo. I was in awe of her little hand, her feet and she smelled so sweet, like the Hershey kiss that she was. Junior came into the room, I don't know from where, but he was mad. I asked him what was the matter and he started to rant and I knew I saw this look before. I sat quietly not listening to what he was saying, because I didn't want to comment on what he was saying. UH OH too late I said something and he slapped the yogurt out of my hand and it flew all over my child. I looked at Candace who started to cry and I didn't hear anything he had to say. My baby needed me. *Fuck* him. I got up to take Candace upstairs to clean her and he made it like it was his idea. He ordered me to clean the shit off of Candace.

Okay let it be his idea.

He followed me upstairs, yelling at me, but all I heard was Candace. I laid her in the crib and when I turned around the beating began. I received blows to my face, my arms, my stomach and I thought *nigga I just had a baby.* I fell to the floor to protect my stomach and that is when he stomped me. I couldn't believe it. The motherfucker just stomped me.

That was it. Somebody was going to die today.

As I lied there clearing my head, he began yelling at me to go downstairs and clean up the shit that he caused. I got to my feet but instead of going downstairs, I went into the bedroom and got the knife that was under my mattress. I came back into the nursery and told him that I was going to clean up my daughter and if he wanted the shit cleaned up down stair he was going to have to do it his damned self.

I thought, did that just come out of me?

Where is this coming from?

Could this be strength?

I realized that my child had given me powers that I didn't know I had.

He started to push me and I resisted. I was trying to get up the nerve to strike but I couldn't and I wondered, *where did that power go*? He pushed me again and again I resisted. I began to get angry and with my back to him, he pushed me again and with one smooth motion I grab the knife that I had hidden in my pants and I intended to sink it right into his heart. The madness had to stop and I was ready to end it but that nigga was so mean and hateful that when I turned I saw a fist headed toward my face that was intended for the back of my head. I ended up stabbing him in his arm and the look on his face was priceless.

I stared at him with death in my eyes. This was supposed to be my new life; a life without abuse of any kind foreign and domestic. I was not about to be a victim yet again. Fuck that shit. I stood there looking at him then I heard Candace crying, as this weak ass nigga cowered in the corner asking me what did I do. What did I do? I had a hickey the size of a walnut on my forehead and my face was swollen. My face had started coming back to life after the birth of Candace and this nigga is doing this. WHAT DID I DO? I had had it.

I went to grab Candace but he had got to her before I did. I ran down the stairs to the door. I stared to panic. Where did my power go? I got the door unlocked with Junior in hot pursuit. I ran to the manager's apartment. I was banging on the door trying to get someone to open it quickly because he was just feet away from me with Candace in his arms.

As the door opened, I rushed in and the Manager saw Junior bleeding and took the baby and I jumped up and slammed the door.

SAFE!

I was breathing hard and had a million questions thrown at me. I just looked up and all the questions were answered. My face looked like I was in a fight with Muhammad Ali and I had just had a baby a month ago.

Angry didn't describe how I felt. Betrayal, hate, sorrow and bewilderment. I was in a low place and I was alone. Correction I was alone with Candace. I called my brother and he reluctantly came to get me because his wife told him that I was his sister and that I needed him. Ain't that bout a bitch? My own brother had to be talked into coming to help his little sister. My family.

My brother drove an LTD and when he got to the apartment I got into the car and LTD(The music group) was playing on the car stereo all I could do but laugh. He liked LTD a little too much. When my brother saw my face he asked me what did I have to be laughing for and I told him I was alive. I had been able to go back to the apartment and get some things, enough to survive and I left.

I rode in the car silently. I had so many things going through my mind and no clue what to do. I got to my mother's house and quickly felt that I was not welcomed. I called my sister in Illinois and she said I could come and stay with her and her husband and five kids.

I convinced my mother to let me stay until I got my Welfare check on the 1st and I would be out of her hair. My brothers were welcomed but I wasn't. I was alone.

The bus ride on Greyhound was fifty-two hours. I had a lot of time to think of what I had been through and what I was going to do to get out of it. I had no clue. I was eighteen, unemployed and an unwed mother. This was my life.

My middle sister, Deidra picked me up from the bus depot. It wasn't a city but a town I saw. Decatur IL. I expected a horse and buggy to pass me any minute. I had nerves of my thoughts. I was homeless. At that thought, I quickly got grateful and hugged my sister when I saw her. We soon made it to her home and as I sat down to catch my breath the ball dropped.

"Is it true that you had an abortion?" Deidra asked in bogus incredulity.

I was mortified. Here I sat in a born again Christian's house and she was asking if I had done the unthinkable. I lied and told her that the test later came up negative and that I wasn't pregnant after all. I thought to myself, *how could my older sister betray me*? She said it would be our little secret.

I stayed to myself and cared for my baby. I had a lot to think about.

What next?

I needed to apply for Welfare and find a job. I didn't have much money and formula wasn't cheap. My sister helped as she could but she had five mouths to feed and I didn't want to be a burden on her.

In the month that I was there, I knew that this was not going to work. The town was too slow, the people was too slow and even though I didn't had more that a high school education, I had common sense and I didn't see much of that here. I was also talking to Junior, who was begging me to come back and that all would be forgiven.

With desperation, I decided to go back. I didn't want to raise Candace by myself. I remember how my mother struggled to care for her family alone and I didn't want Candace to grow up without her father so I choose to go back. I was alone and he was the only one who wanted me.

Chapter 12

Junior met me at the bus stop at Grand central in downtown Los Angeles. I was back in the city. He wore a black shiny shirt and black polyester pants. My man, his dark skin was so rich and his teeth were white. He had an air about him that yelled confidence and I wanted it. I hugged him for what seemed like a long time and he smelled so good. I couldn't wait to get back to the house after all that phone sex we had while I was away. I had plans. I was going to put it on him so good that he was going to be afraid to lose me and we will be happy.

Yea right!

The sex was intense and I got my first orgasm. I didn't mind that my knees were on my forehead. I mirrored his freakiness to insure that Candace and I would be taken care of. I thought I had made a difference and that he now saw my value. I cooked and he taught me how to do laundry. I would read his text books while he was at work so I would have something to talk to him about. I still received the occasional mental abuse. *You're too fat, don't smile, you look funny, even the bacon was fried too hard.*

One day, I opened his mail and it was his checking account. I figured we were a family and I had a right to know how we were doing. I was trying to understand everything that he knew and so that I would understand when he talked to me about things. I ran across a check with this woman's name on it. When he got home I asked him about it and he went off. I had no idea that I had done anything wrong.

Boy was I wrong.

He back handed me across my face and I landed on the other side of the room. I didn't know what was happening. I thought it was a legitimate question as he was on top of me beating the shit out of me. As I tried desperately to shield my face, all I could think was that I guess the sex wasn't good enough. Even while I was getting my ass whooped, I still had a sense of humor.

Wait a minute, I thought, in that instant, my mind went to Candace and the power came back. I started fighting him back. Blow for blow I stood toe to toe. I was raised with five brothers in my house and I fought at least three of them. I knew how to fight, I just chose not to fight in my home, but he didn't care and I stopped caring too.

"For this fight!"

He was a Black belt in karate but I had fear and anger and the safety of Candace on my mind. He fell on the floor and I jumped on top of him and did what Tina did to Ike. While lying on the floor, he throw his hands over his head and started to moan as if he was getting off on me whooping his ass. How disgusting, the nigga was sick. I got off of him and told him he was a sad son of a bitch. *Eagle Scout, my ass.* What was wrong with him? I thought he was different. I had no idea he was that bad off. He got up and ran out the door and left it open as if I was going to run after him. I simply slammed the door and thought *what a punk ass motherfucker*.

All of the sudden the door exploded. That nigga had put both fists through the front door. What the fuck!

I did say he had a black belt in Karate.

The manager came to the apartment and calmed him down like she was a snake charmer. A white trailer park trash white woman not like the blond haired, blue eyed beautiful woman I saw on TV. Who knew she was one of many fucking my man? That nigga was more public than a port-a-potty.

Just nasty!

He settled down and from the way she caressed his face, I thought, *What is this shit?* I've been hoodwinked, bamboozled. The more I watched, the madder I got. I'm not going anywhere, I'm not running. The gauntlet was thrown. It was time to fuck him up. I didn't care about a family; all I cared about was vindication. I looked at the manager and said enough of this shit. Fix the damn door and went back into the apartment.

I didn't care anymore. I had no trust and I was determined to mirror his hatefulness and I became mean. If he wanted to fight, I was going to fight. I discovered that not caring was liberating.

That apartment was my house and I set that rules. When he threw a tantrum I would look at him as if to say who gives a shit and just walk away. Sometimes he would buck and we fought, but most of the time he just cowered in shame. I would scrub the floors to repent from being so mean. How much more of this can I take? When he would say I was fat, I would bake a chocolate cake and it eat as to say who gives a fuck. When he said I looked funny because of the results of the Bell Palsy I would laugh like I was mentally challenged. I was tired of being victimized but being like this was not making me feel good either.

Candace was now fifteen months old and she was walking. I always made time for her in this chaos and she was often asleep when he got home just in case he was in one of his fighting moods. One day that was not the case. He came home all fired up and I was not in the mood.

He was trying to get a rise out of me and I was just not interested. I was tired of the teeth marks on his penis that I did not put there. The late night karate practices where he was fucking the female instructor. The put downs, fist fights were wearing down my spirit. This was not my life and I was just tired of him, but where was I to go? What was I to do? As a child I felt invisible and now as a young adult I felt like a sparring partner. This was not my life.

When he put his hands on me, I just lost it. I socked him in his jaw and told him to back up off me. That's all it took and we were there fighting in front of Candace and it didn't faze her not one bit. My mother instincts took over and I kept the fight contained away from her so that she wouldn't get hurt. He stopped and went away and then I ran to the phone and called his father

"You need to get over here, Junior done lost his mind" is all I said.

His father knew what that meant…

He still remembers the time that I brought Junior to the house because he had tried to kill himself by ingesting a whole bottle of Tylenol. His mother was a nurse and she would know what to do I thought. On the way to the house I told him that if he wanted to die I would help him. I was speeding down the street at ninety miles per hours running stop signs and laughing. He was scared shitless and I was mad as hell.

When we got to his parent's house, it was hard getting him out of the car. It took his mother, father and me to drag his sorry ass to the shower and then he shattered the shower door into a million pieces.

That nigga knew how to get attention.

I looked at the mess he had made and I went numb. I felt bad that I had brought him over here and now he was destroying their house. I thought, What I'm I going to do?

I sat down on the sofa in the same room that his date for the Eagle scout ceremony sat in. She was smarter than me, I thought. While his mother was tending to him his father came out to ask me what had happened. I looked at him with sorrowful eyes and said your guess is as good as mind.

I really wanted to say "You raised a punk ass nigga that needs a titty," but I had respect for my elders. I heard wrestling and vomiting going on and I just closed my eyes so no one would see them rolling. That fool was getting on my nerves, but I still loved him. Or did I just pity him? I knew he was going through something but denial was a son of a bitch. I don't know how long it was before he came into the living room like nothing had happened.

I guess he got that titty.

I sat there listening to a lecture from two dysfunctional alcoholics with nine messed up children and I was trying to save one from the litter. I sat there and waited for his command to go then we were off back home to chaos and much needed sleep…

So his father knew and was over there in a hurry. Junior came out of nowhere with a belt like he was going to whoop me with a belt.

This nigga done lost his mind.

I grabbed the belt and he stood there lost. I thought, all I wanted to do was love him but I had reduced him to a man that was in serious need of psychological help. I picked up Candace and walked out of the apartment and got into the van. His sister was there and she took Candace and thank God she did.

Junior came out wielding a butcher knife and his father tried to talk to him but stepped out of the way. Junior jumped in the van and I thought this was it, but he handed me the knife and put it up to his chest. I didn't want to hurt him I just wanted peace and a family, but what I got is misery.

I could hear my mother saying "You done jumped out of the frying pan into the fire." I quickly threw the knife out of the van and it nicked his father because his punk ass was trying to see what Junior was going to do.

Can I get some help here?

Junior's father finally got him out of the van and we left. I didn't want him to feel defeated and kill us all.

I stayed with his parents because I was too ashamed to call my family and I knew that they would not have helped me. I was alone.

While I was at his parents' house, Junior would often come by the house. I would talk to him but I was scared. I wasn't ready to die. God had other plans for my life and this was not it.

The fear of no money, nowhere to go and the feeling that no one will love me, cause me to go back. He had moved from the old apartment, probably because the trailer park trash manager now knew his secrets. The apartment was swank. Full length mirrors in the bedroom, pool area and social lounge. It didn't look like children belonged there and Candace and I were not on the lease. I knew this was not going to last long. I played along in hopes that he came to his senses. That was not to happen.

One night I was at home with Candace and she was already asleep. She was a good baby and sleep through the night. Junior came home and took a shower and I asked where he was going. He said that he was going to play pool downstairs. I told him that I would like to go and he started making noise and woke Candace up. I look in the mirror and his dumb ass was smiling not know that I could see his reflection. Did the nigga think he was a vampire and didn't have a reflection?

I told him that he was full of shit. If he didn't want me to come all he had to do was say so. He pulled me into the bathroom and slapped me.

Big mistake.

The bathroom was a small space and he could do none of that Kung Fu bullshit in there. I socked him in his jaw again and this time he fell on the toilet. I was going to make it to where he didn't want to come back to me.

I drilled on his face like I was born and raised in Watts.

Oh I was!

That nigga didn't know what hit him. I got

satisfaction in whooping that ass. He was whimpering like a little girl and I just lost all respect, admiration and pity. This was it and it was no turning back, so what the fuck. I went for what I knew and I knew a lot of street shit. I was born and raised in the hood. *WESTSIDE!*

He was so shocked that he tried to get out of the bathroom, but I was against the door.

I guess my big ass was good for something.

I told him, as I beat the shit out of him that it wasn't that I didn't know how to fight. It was that I didn't want to fight in my home. I wanted to be a good role model for my daughter. I didn't want her to grow up in violence and it was obvious that this was the only thing he knew. Junior pushed me back and tried to slap me. He grazed my cheek as he tried to run out of the bathroom with his hand trailing behind him and I slammed the door and caught four digits. He squealed like the swine that he was and I almost pissed my pants laughing. When I came out of the bathroom he was gone and Candace had fell back to sleep. I wondered if I was too late. That child slept through all that violence.

I packed Candace and my clothes and shoes in a duffle bag and took the change out of the jar on the counter and locked the door.

Candace and I sat at the Bus stop in Pomona to catch the 494, or 490 bus to Los Angeles. It was September 1981, I sat there and tried to make sense of the decisions I made in my live and thought about the thing I learned skills being with that Jerk. I can drive a stick, I know my way around freeways, I know how to do laundry. I know how to write a check, I know how to conduct business at a Bank, my grammar is better than it was and I know when enough is enough

The bus came just in time and I got on like the homeless person that I was. I explained to the driver that I didn't know if I had enough. He asked where I was going in L.A. I told him Manchester and Normandie, which were the cross streets.

I considered the bus driver my first angel. He wrote something on the transfer and told me to show it to any driver and I was get to where I was going. I thanked him and sat quietly. He tried to strike a conversation, but I couldn't tell him my sob story. At the time I didn't want to hear it myself. I felt pathetic, and it was the last time with the toad.

Chapter 12

By the time we made it to Los Angeles, I was exhausted. Candace was a good baby and I held her tight from the elements of the night air. She was a twenty-one month old bundled in a blanket sleeper and her little face peeked out. She slept most of the trip which gave me time to figure out my next move.

The transfer worked great and I was able to get to Normandie and at that time Santa Barbara which is now Martin Luther King Blvd. I felt that I couldn't go on. I called my mother from a pay phone at 3:30 in the morning and she sounded agitated when she found out it was me. I asked her if she would come to get me. She had assumed that I was still in Pomona, but I quickly told her that I was down the street. That didn't seem to matter, but I pleaded with disappointment if she could just come and get her daughter and her baby granddaughter from the dark cold night.

By the time my mother came to get us I was numb. I couldn't understand how a mother could be so cruel. Okay, I messed up, but how long was I going to have to pay for my mistake. I needed her help and all

I got was more grief.

I got in the car and said nothing. I didn't want to talk about what had happened and it shown on my face. It was swollen and I was red. My eyes were puffy and I was exhausted.

We finally made it to the house and my mother gave me the indication that I was not welcomed. She said things like Henry said that two women can't live under the same roof.

I got the message.

I couldn't sleep and my little brother Kevin stayed up with me. I kept checking on Candace because I worried about how all this would affect her. She was my only concern and I wanted to give her a better life than I had.

The telephone rang.

It was five in the morning.

It was Junior, crying and begging me to come back. I told him that I was through. This madness had gone on too long. He was crying loud and Kevin was on the bed cracking up. Junior heard him laughing and then it started. He called me a bitch and that I was nothing but shit and I replied, "Shit without you is better than being shit with you." and hung up.

My mother got up and came to Kevin's room, I apologized for the language because my mother had never heard me talk like that and I was embarrassed and ashamed. I was sick of him affecting my life. This had to be over. I asked my mother to let me stay until I could make other arrangement and she reluctant but she agreed. I called Deidra in Illinois and she agreed to let me stay with her again.

Before I left for Illinois, Melanie threw me a going away party. We did that from time to time and at these things, I felt that I was the odd man out, this time it felt different. It felt like I was with family and they

were truly sad to see me go, but I had to leave. I had to go to recover from all that I had been through with Junior. We had a lot of food. Barbeque, potato salad, baked beans and I made my famous peach cobbler. I felt that Melanie and I were the closes we had ever been then the ball dropped.

The evening was winding down and people starting to leave. Melanie notice's and quickly got everyone together to make a toast. We all held our glasses up to receive the toast and she began.

"I know that Marilyn has to leave and I understand it but I don't like it. I already lost one sister who is out of the state and Marilyn is leaving. I just want you to know that I will miss you but you got to do what you got to do. I just hate the bastard for making you leave. He (Junior) use to come to my job at the convalescent hospital and pick up one of a girl that worked with me and she use to talk about how freaky he was. I hate that bastard."

As I heard the toast, my glass slowly descended and I was shocked. All I could think about was that she knew that but didn't tell me and then she spill it with an audience. What did I do to this girl to want to hurt me this bad.

Everyone begin to look at me and I was so embarrassed and hurt that I ran out of the house. I started to cry. Melanie knew and didn't say a word. *How long had this been going on?* I thought. Why did she have to say it in front of family and friends? What was the point? I tried to justify her actions, but there was no justification. She was wrong and heartless, but what did I ever do to make her want to hurt me like this. I began to get angry and I started crying. My mother came out just in time because I was about to go back in there and whoop her ass. I was about to show her my ghetto side. The side I tried so hard to run away from but she had took me there.

My mother calmed me down and I didn't want to act crazy in her presence, so I stopped crying and went into my special place of peace. I became silent and I just stared off while my mother spoke. I can't remember what she said, but she was confident that her words calmed me down.

Another fifty-two hours on the Greyhound. Enough time to think of what I left behind. All the misery, from Melanie and Junior, and the feeling of invisibility. Deidra was waiting for me this time and I didn't get a chance to think about the small town, but I think it was more than that. I was really through with that chapter in my life. It was truly time to move on and I had made my mind up that that was what I was going to do.

Deidra and I arrived to her home and it was different. My sister had to move because she needed more space with five children. It was a nice house and I was grateful for her to take me in again.

As I walked in the house, I noticed that she could use my help. I could tell that she was struggling. She showed me where I was going to sleep and said that Candace could share her daughter's room. I felt good that she had made a place for me even though it was a storage room. It was mine. I unpacked and got Candace settled down and we ate dinner.

The kids were settled down for bed and Deidra's questions began. I told the story and confessed that I had had three abortions and then I apologized for lying the first time she had asked me. She was interested in all that I had been through and I watched her fascination, but I wondered if it was concern or something to gossip about. At this point I didn't care; I had a place to stay.

I helped her with the children and the house work. We had a relationship and I enjoyed it. I finally had a sister that I could talk to and that made me realized that I never had this before. Both of my sister's left home soon after the death of my father and ended up married to older abusive men.

I started to get an eye infection and Deidra took me to the doctor. The doctor stated that I had a venereal disease and I said in my eye. The only one that I had ever had sex with was Junior. They gave me medication and it soon went away but came back after the medication was gone. I went back to the doctor and they gave me more medication for Gonorrhea. I didn't think I had it but I went through the humiliating looks from Deidra and the nurse who came in with the big horse pills. I asked her what they were for and she said "You know what they're for." In my mind I say fuck it and took the drugs to get rid of it. Deidra was looking at me like I had something she was afraid her family would catch. I felt dirty and ashamed. I thought I'm tired and this shit. I called Junior to tell him what the doctor said and the nigga accused me of fooling around. What a joke. The port-a-potty man. Whatever.

I went to Deidra and explained that I thought it was the lack of housekeeping that caused the eye irritation and she was pissed. She made me help her clean the house from top to bottom. I didn't mind especially when I found out that the *brown* carpet was actually red. The medication or the house cleaning worked and I thought I'm glad to have gotten over that. My sister stopped looking at me like I was diseased and life went on. I was proud that we cleaned the house and I was admiring our hard work when my brother in law came home from work and walked tar all over our hard work. I told him to take off his shoes because we had just cleaned the carpet and he told me that it was his house and he would do as he pleased. I went to my room and didn't say another word.

This is not my life, I thought and went into my chant. I'm grown and I need to do something.

But what?

I never went anywhere.

I didn't know anyone.

I only had a high school diploma from a failed school system and no work experience. I realized I had not got out of the gate and my race had already started. I was late. Just like a condiment, I needed to ketchup.

I was there for two months and it was November. Deidra was preparing a party for her husband's birthday and I was helping. She had baked a cake and we needed a table to put it on. She found a table and pulled it apart to insert the leaf to make it bigger. Roaches began to run everywhere. I picked Candace up off the floor and Deidra ran to get the bugs spray and the question was answered. My eyes blew up like I was on Mars like in the movie the Total Recall. I covered my face and ran to my room.

I began packing and I called the bus depot and Candace and I were on the Greyhound before the party started and we headed back to California. I didn't know what I was going to do but I knew Illinois was not where I was going to do it.

Fifty two hours later, arrived at Grand

Central station. I was tired and needed a shower. The only luggage was a foot locker that had everything that I possessed. I saw my mother and was happy to see her. I wanted to get to the car, so that I could take a shower when we got to my mother's house. My mother decided to take the bus, public transportation to pick me up. I was agitated and I tried not to let it show. I couldn't bring my foot locker and I wanted a shower. What was she thinking? Or should I say what was she trying to tell me. We left the bus station and I just followed my mother. I indicated that we were getting on the wrong bus when my mother informed me that she was going to Hollywood park. I thought, Hollywood park are you kidding me?. I guess the message was loud and clear. I couldn't stay at her house. I told her that I need to get to a phone and find out where I was going to live and I would like to go to her house and get to looking. My mother was reluctant and looking at me like I was a squatter threatening never to leave once I arrived. I assured my mother that I understood that I couldn't live with her.

But my unemployed brothers could.

We finally arrived at my mother's house and I immediately got on the phone. I was calling some numbers in the phone book and Charles came in. I wave to greet him because I was still on the phone. When I got off the phone he asked me what I was doing and when I told him he exploded. "My baby sister is not going to be living in no motel!" He had a look I knew too well. Light colored skin, wavy hair and a stare that was fierce. He asked his wife if he could take Candace and me in to help me get on my feet and she agreed. I was relieved and truly grateful. My hero came to my rescue again.

He took us home and made arrangements to get my footlocker.

Chapter 13

The next morning, Sue, Charles's wife, Charles and I had a meeting and the ground rules were set. They gave me sixty days to get it together. I was to save my Welfare money and they would buy Candace's and my needs.

Charles was always the one that came to my rescue. He was the parent when my mother mentally went ghost. He taught me how to cook and he gave me a philosophy. He would say things like *it cost to live in this world*, and *If you bump your head on a brick wall once it's okay, but if you do it again you are stupid.* Charles and I would debate many issues.

He would make me think like I was in training for life. And I was

Sue was a wonderful woman. I looked up to her like a mentor. She was soft spoken and understanding. I needed her in my life. She was an angel and I appreciated her. I felt that God had given me the sister I needed and I was grateful. She would give me words of encouragement and she always knew when I needed it.

November 1981 was a start of my new life. I could see the light at the end of the tunnel. I lived with the one sibling who I trusted not to hurt me. He wanted me to succeed and he knew that I had made mistakes, but he didn't hold them against me. I would wake up every morning and clean his home, not because he told me that I had to do it but because I was grateful. I made sure that his kitchen was clean when he got home so that he could come home and cook the fabulous food that he always prepared. I would clean the bathroom and vacuum the carpet. I never once went into his bedroom which I felt was sacred. He and Sue allowed me the opportunity to get back on my feet and I wanted them to know how much I appreciated it.

They had gave me sixty days to get it together and I was ready in

forty five days. I went to him and told him that I was ready to move. He informed me that I had two more weeks. I told him that I had enrolled in the community college and that I had gotten a studio apartment right down stairs from him. It looked like he was not ready to let me go, but he knew it was time. He gave me the option of a refrigerator or $200. I took the money because I could get a cheaper fridge and use the rest off the money on necessities for my first place.

My first place was perfect. The rent was cheap and it was enough space for Candace and I. I moved on January 15, 1982, Martin Luther King's birthday, my day of liberation. I had two weeks before I would be starting school. I had registered and the financial aid was completed. I just had to get my head clear from all the garbage that was in it.

Since I've been back, Junior came by once on the pretense that he wanted to see his child. My brother let it be known that he was not welcomed. His sister had told me that he had gotten engaged in October. I thought, ain't that bout a bitch since I left him in September. Here it is November, I had been back in California for two weeks went he came to my brother's home trying to talk in this mack daddy voice like he still cared for me. He didn't know that I knew about the engagement when I asked him "So when is the big day?" He looked shocked and tried to deny it. I told him that I was through and left him outside with Candace so that he could visit with her. It was a short visit, because it took all of fifteen minutes for him to knock on my brother's door to give her back.

Good ridden!

I had to get childcare for Candace so I could go to school and I thought my mother would watch her. Boy was I wrong. Charles also said that *assumption will only make an ass out of you* and it did. I was now desperate. Who was I going to get to watch Candace?

I had no time to wonder about why my mother refused although I was a little hurt. I did find a low income daycare center close to where my mother worked. I didn't have a car, so Public transportation was my Godsend. I didn't complain. I had no time. I had to keep my focus and that was school. I was doing this for myself, but Candace gave me the power and God gave me the strength to endure the many challenges that I faced. I found that I leaned on the word of God to get through a lot of the pain that I had. I knew He had my back. The bus driver, my brother, Charles, and the daycare center. I had to catch a bus three times a week to take Candace to the daycare center that was six miles out the way. I used the time to teach Candace things that we saw while on the bus. It became our little adventure.

One day while I was taking Candace to the daycare center, I saw my cousin with her two girls going into the family hardware store where my mother worked. I stopped in only to find out that my mother was watching her two little girls. I couldn't be mad. They treated my mother like the hired help and it only mad me mad at the abuse that my mother had to endure.

I knew I had to keep my focus and that is what I did. I studied hard and I got through the remedial classes and was now ready to get into the meat of my studies which was Accounting. I loved numbers and I enjoyed the classes. I was different here than I was in high school. I was working towards a goal to achieve a dream of success and a better life for Candace and myself.

I remember a time when I seduced a man to get Junior off my mind. It did hurt that he had gotten engaged so soon after I left him and I felt that I still had his scent on me. He had been my first love and I felt that he still had a hold on me. I was hard. I treated men how they had treated woman for so long. Loved them and leaved them. No, I was not bad. I dictated who I would sleep with, not them choosing me. I only did it when the pain was too great which was not than often. The memory that I had given my Hope diamond to a frog was a horrible one. A wannabe white boy, a double stuffed Oreo, a fake Eagle scout who didn't deserve the honor.

Junior would bring his new wife when he would visit Candace. I think that he thought that he was rubbing it in my face, but I thanked God that she made him unavailable. I still loved him and I had now realized that he was gone. I never showed my feelings. I was the best hostess.

When Candace was three, Junior and his wife Sharon, came to get Candace for the weekend. This was the first time that Candace and I would be apart. I was afraid to be alone, but I let her go.

Sharon was dress like a hooker in her Candies shoes and her halter top and tight jeans. Her finger nails were painted some God awful color that you shouldn't ever be in the house of God with. I thought to myself, that was once me. I praise God for that deliverance. Sharon became one of my angels that kept him away from me.

I made it through Friday night alone without Candace and it was hard. The next morning I met a guy on the bus and brought him back to my place. I had a rule that you couldn't come over unless you were invited. I fucked his brains out and then dismissed him only to find out that he had left part of himself with me. No, not disease thank God but the dirt on my sheet from his back was sickening. I had to get it together.

This was not me. I was a child of God and I know he was not pleased with my behavior. I took a shower for what felt like hours and then I hit the books. I had to keep my mind off of Candace. I hope that she was safe and that she was treated with love. I stopped studying to pray for my child and cast my cares, I also repented for my fornicating behavior. My focus came back and the rest of the weekend was quiet and alone.

Junior brought Candace back on Sunday and asked to use the bathroom. I obliged and began talking to my angel Sharon. She told me that Candace was a good girl and that she would call her mom. I told Sharon that she was Candace's mom and that it didn't bother me. I told her that it was comforting to know that they got along well. Junior stormed out of the bathroom and rushed her out of the apartment I couldn't do nothing but laugh and Candace laughed too not knowing why. Junior was pissed because I was not jealous. He was so predictable.

Life goes on!

After the experience with dirty boy, I set my sight much higher. I never like bad boys so I stayed away from them. My oldest brother Rodney would tell me that you don't bring wolves to your sheep. I was young when he told me that, but I came to understand that. I didn't want any wolves in Candace's life or mine so they were off limits. I met a nice guy named Michael and I would speak about my dreams and how I intended to live. One day we were together and I saw a Mercedes 250 SL. It was sleek, shiny and sported and I said one day I will be in that. On our next date, Michael took me out in a royal blue Mercedes 250 SL. It was great but it wasn't mine. I guess I should have been more specific. He took me to Westwood and saw a movie. I had a nice time and the perfect date turned into sex at my place. I felt that I moved up from dirty sheet boy and this was a move in the right direction. I was beginning to have feelings for Michael and I was thinking of introducing him to Candace and then he disappeared.

Weeks had gone by and I felt duped. Niggas, how did that get by me? I know the hunt was over. He had scored and I was the prize and now the conquest was over. I thought he got me, chalk one for him. I was still learning and that will never happen twice but it still hurt and I didn't like pain, emotional or physical.

Michael finally showed up uninvited and Candace was not home, she was with her father who would occasional play daddy. I was in the kitchen washing dishes and he tapped on the window. I had time to get myself together and to deal with this motherfucker. I went to the door and asked why he didn't call first for an invite. He knew the rules, but like most niggas they like to change the rules or see if they can. I let him in and decided to play the game. We talked and I told him that I was worried about him. I had him eating out of my hands, but he was about to be served alright. We started kissing and he began to feel me up. I played that game and talked about how much I missed him and still he never offered up an explanation as to where he had gone. He started to undress me and I let him. I told him to take off his clothes so that I could see his beautiful body. Okay, I stroked his ego a little. After we were both naked I stood over him and told him he could pay me now. He looked at me with this puzzled look on his face. I looked him square in his face and told if he was going to treat me like a prostitute he was going to pay me like one. He started to shudder and I looked at him like nigga please. I left the room and got a big scarf and wrapped it around my size 14 body covering my 38 triple D's. with hips to match. I was called thick. Meat on my bones but in all the right places. I went back in the room and he was getting dressed. I thought look at this broke down nigga. He didn't take time to know who I was. I didn't play that shit. If you are not willing to stay don't try to play. I wasn't a hoe nor was I going to be treated like one. I told him that I didn't know what kind of woman he was used to dealing with but I wasn't the one and he left.

Good ridden! Another nigga bites the dust. I was pissed, but not sad for some reason. I guess my point was well taken but not and I didn't care. I got the point and that's all that mattered. Men were spoiled and woman let them have their way but not me.

Chapter 14

Junior brought Candace back and I guess I was still in a mood from Michael. I was hot and bothered and when he started paying me compliments I say What the hell? I will play his game. I put Candace down for a much needed nap and took Junior in the hallway between the living area and the bathroom of my studio apartment and fucked his brains out. I asked him if he missed it and he moaned in ecstasy and I thought, *this dumb bastard* but I did have fun. I was able to release the pent up angry from Michael and I gave him my all.

After that, Junior became a permanent fixture on the weekends. He would take Candace and I out to eat and shopping. He even paid for her 4th birthday party. What the heck, Candace had her daddy and he was a good standby. I reasoned with myself that it was alright and that I had him before Sharon and this was payback for what she did to me. I didn't want him to come back to me; I just wanted to have a good time and his presence for Candace.

Junior came by and he was kind of in a mood. I didn't ask him what the problem was, that was Sharon's duty not mine. He pulled out of his pocket a ring box and opened it. He went on to tell me he had it to get it cleaned and that it should have been on my finger. I told him that it didn't because the ring that was supposed to be on my finger was a solitaire not some diamond chipped cocktail ring and he looked at me wounded but it was not my responsibility to stroke him. Candace sat quietly coloring in her book as if all was well and that's all that mattered.

Junior was slowly moving in when I notice that he started spending the nights on weekdays. I asked him how did Sharon feel about him not coming home at night and he said she would be mad but would get over it. I told him fuck that shit not me. As we lay naked in the bed, I asked him if he think that he would ever hit me again and he said he didn't know. I look at him and told him that I have got to get me a gun. He asked me why and I told him that I will kill him dead before I let him hit me again and I didn't blink. He got up, got dressed, and left.

Later, he came back and told me that he and Sharon were not doing well and that I was the one he wanted. He talked about how she spent too much money trying to keep up with the Jones's whoever they were. That she didn't know how to cook and she was hiding credit card statements and that he was so far in debt.

Ah, he realized he had it good.

Junior said that he would never put his hands on me in the wrong way and I thought, you better not. He asked me if he could come and live with us. What the hell, he was her father and I enjoyed his company. I soon discovered being the other woman was better than being the woman to a psychopath. The going out stopped and the tantrums started but he knew he better not hit me. We were in an argument one day and he called me a bitch. I saw red. No one called me a bitch. I told him to pack his shit and be gone when I got back. I took Candace and slammed the door to my apartment and as I did a candle stick came crashing through my picture window. I went to the telephone booth and called the police. How dare he break the window we sleep under. I thought, that was one selfish, sick nigga. If he didn't care about me he should have thought of Candace.

The police was Johnny on the spot. They came quickly because Junior was not finish packing. He began to talk stupid saying I was going to miss his dick and I replied that my five fingers could do more than his dick ever did and the cops started to laugh. The police escorted him out of my apartment and I thought the drama has ended when I notice that my school books were gone. I left Candace in the apartment and ran to the police who were still parked out front. They raced to meet him at the exit gate and I ran to catch up to them. That lying bastard tried to say that he bought my books and that he choose not to let me keep them. I explained to the police that I got the books from a book loan and it was stamped in every book. One of the officers open the book and in bold red letters read BOOK LOAN. The officer shook his head and took all the books

and gave them to me. I took the books and thanked them and turn around and left. I was not interested in what they had to say to him.

It was over.

I would continue with my studies, and take Candace out to play outside. I felt it was good to spend a lot of time with her, something that I didn't receive from my own mother. I bathe her every night and tucked her into bed. I read her bedtime stories and gave her lots of hugs and kisses. I gave her balanced meals and taught her how to eat. I was determined to give Candace a good life and an education would assure that.

I started getting headaches and I thought I

needed glasses because my sight would get weak and tear up. I went to the doctor at Martin Luther King or should I say Killer King which is what most people would call it. I was diagnosed with a Pseudo tumor in my brain.

Haven't I been through enough?

My mind fell on Candace and I was scared. She only had a part time daddy who only came around to see if I was hot or cold. My mother would not watch Candace while I went to school so I knew it would be out of the question and I needed to be admitted into the hospital. I called my brother Kevin and told him that he would have use of my car if he would watch Candace while I was in the hospital. I knew that I didn't want her to stay with Melanie and Daddy Clyde, the pedophile. I hadn't forgotten what he tried to do.

Kevin agreed to watch Candace and dropped me off at the hospital. While they waited to get me admitted, I had a chance to find out why they called it Killer King. The mistreatment of patients, the dirty floors, and the bad attitudes of the employees. I got up and ripped the hospital band off of my wrist and the doctor asked what I was doing. I told him that I couldn't do this. He told me that I could die and I told him it would not be at Killer King and left. I called my mother who tore into to me because Kevin had dropped Candace off to her and left in my car. I was mad and hurt at the same time. How was I going to get to my child? I was only there for four hours. Family is a motherfucker. I must be adopted because I didn't understand how they could be so heartless. They knew I had a brain tumor and that didn't even matter.

I was all alone.

I sat there for I don't know how long at that hospital waiting for Kevin to bring my car and Candace back to me. All I thought about was what the doctor said about death. I prayed to God that he would give me more time. I didn't want Candace to go through what I had been through and I felt comforted. Kevin returned to the hospital and if looks could kill, he was already six feet under. I got in the car and didn't even have to tell him to get out of the driver's seat. He tried to explain but I wasn't hearing it. I trusted him and he betrayed me. I thought I could count on him, but I assumed wrong yet again.

I was angry at myself for trying to force love and concern on my family when time after time they had let me down. I didn't want to keep going to Charles with my problems.

After I dropped Kevin back at my mother's home, I went home. I put Candace down for a nap and went into the bathroom and cried and prayed and prayed and cried. I was exhausted but I was determined to find someone to take whatever was in my head out. I got the yellow pages and was lead to Dr. Biggers my next angel.

Chapter 15

Dr. Biggers was a young, good looking, black man in his forties and he had an office on Santa Rosalia near Crenshaw, I think. He asked me question like he knew exactly what was happening and I was amazed but still leery. He was black. I didn't know that black people had positions like this. He was a doctor in a nice area and he took Medi-Cal. I was admitted immediately into White Memorial Hospital and Junior's sister Kathy took me to the hospital and agreed to watch Candace, she was an angel. She stayed at my apartment so Candace would not be scared. She often brought Candace to the hospital to see me. I was there for a week and they were my only visitors. I spent my time reading the Book of Job in the bible. I wanted to know what I was going through and why? I was comforted and was now ready for the procedure. It was a spinal tap. I had to get my brain drained. What I had was water on the brain from over the counter diet aids that ended in trim…

A white man came into the room and I must admit that I was a little relieved that he was going to do the procedure. I didn't have too much confidence in the black man even though he was handsome. I was in the fetal position and I was ready to go through whatever I had to get well and back to Candace. The white doctor caused me so much pain and I started to scream when my leg involuntarily shot out in front of me. He pulled the needle out of my back and Dr. Biggers came running into the room to calm me down. After I was quieted, Dr. Biggers did the procedure without pain or incident. I felt stupid and ashamed but I also realized that the media and television had lied to me.

Black people were intelligent and could be doctor, lawyers or whatever they wanted to be. We were not confined to being trash men, janitors, drug dealers, pimps or unemployed. I begin to get angry at myself for believing the lies of television and the media had fed me. Dr. Biggers became an angel in more ways than one.

I was released with a clean bill of health and a new found lease on life. The experience was both cleansing and informative. I learn a good lesson about my ability and I could no longer be lied to by television or other's opinions. I left the hospital a different woman, a woman of possibilities.

Kathy ended up moving in with me and we shared the rent which meant more money for me. She had a son closed to Candace's age and they were cousins. We had the same morals of child rearing and I was comfortable with her like a sister. I felt God had his ways of giving you what you need and I missed not having a close relationship with my

own sisters. We would teach the children and cook together and after

Junior's last episode, I decided to take a breather from men. I chose to be celibate and I was fine with that. I was on a mission to reach my goal of earning my Associates degree.

Jerry started coming over to my apartment, but it wasn't for me or Candace it was for Kathy and then they became involved. I knew this was not a good idea, because I knew Jerry. It was all about him always. I tried to tell Kathy but she was smitten. Soon Kathy and I were on the outs. She started staying away after Jerry had moved in with us and it was rent time and she dropped a bomb on us. She was not coming back. She had gotten an apartment up stairs from me and wasn't going to pay her share of the rent. I asked her why didn't she tell me her plans so that I could be better prepared and she said nothing. Jerry had a lot to say and I told him just to leave it alone, but I kept her vacuum cleaner as retribution. I saw her baby daddy moving into her apartment and I was glad but we still didn't speak to another. We were family, but I refused to push the issue and continued with my life. Jerry continued to stay with me and he would take Candace to the park and photograph her. She loved her Uncle Jerry and made the mistake and called him daddy. He freaked out. I tried to explain to him that he was her only father figure since Junior hadn't showed his face for months. Jerry was a pothead and he stopped being with Candace. He was high all the time and he would listen to reggae music. I would hit a joint now and then but I wasn't a regular. I didn't like the way it made me look.

I earned my Associates degree in December of '84 and I had no clue what to do next. Charles got me a warehouse job where he worked and I was cool with that for now. While at work, the manager of my apartment called my job and said that Jerry wouldn't let them into the apartment to do some repairs that I had requested. I went home and got Jerry's side of the story.

Nonsense. I told him that he needed to figure out what he was going to do because his workman's comp had ran out and now all the bills fell on me. He told me he would do something and he did. That nigga got me evicted. He cussed the manager out and she was afraid of him and told me I had to leave. I told her that I would put him out but she still said I had to go. I was a good tenant and I didn't understand how this could be happening. I found out that secretly while I was at work Jerry and Kathy had hooked back up and that they were seeing each other when I was at work. As if it made a difference, that was my brother not my lover. I was given a thirty day notice and Jerry took his belonging and began walking up the stairs saying let me see you get out of this. I thought, you heartless bastard. What about Candace? Did he think of her? And Kathy, why would she take him over us?

While at work Charles noticed that something was wrong. By this time he had moved out of the apartment and went to live with my mother to help her out. Kevin was also going through problems and needed a place to stay so Charles decided to move out of the house and give it to Kevin, his wife Jennifer and son and me and Candace. It worked for a while but Kevin and Jennifer parenting skills were a little lacking. I took care of Candace and soon started taking care of their son. I would play with him, read to him and made sure he ate a balance meal. I was often criticized about the way I cared for Candace but what did they know their son often smell like piss because he was a bed wetter.

Jeff, my brother had left his wife and was now living with the woman that took him or should I say the woman that he choose over his wife and son, but that's another story entirely. Anyway, he had a proposition for me. He wanted me to take over his car payment to his Camaro and I needed a car so I agreed. He had bought another car and was paying two car notes so it was a win situation. I had been saving my money and had enough to get the car towed and repaired. I had the car for about two months when my Jeff invited me over for dinner. He was checking out the car and I thought he was looking at how well I took care of it. I was proud of my car or should I say his car. He took me back into the house and began explaining that with insurance, he had to sell the Camaro. I told him that I would get the insurance but he had already made his mine up. He said that he had talked to a dealer who would take it as a trade so his new girlfriend could get the Beamer that she was looking at. I was in shock while he took my keys and proceeded to tell me that I could have her 76 Volkswagen Bug and all I had to do was pay her $700. I had already spent a fortune getting the Camaro running and was never late on my payment and he wanted me to pay more. This nigga must be crazy. I agreed to the conditions because obviously I had no choice. My Camaro was good as gone. I left his house numb and hurt. That was one of my older brothers. They both had jobs better than mine and they did this to me. I was mad as hell.

Family. What a joke!

I got so many question about what happened to the Camaro and I didn't want to discuss it. I told my mother and she said that you should never do business with family. That's it. I wanted her to go to him and tell him what he did was wrong but she was going to stay out of it as usual. I tried to honor the agreement until one day I was driving and I heard clanking then the Bug came to a screeching halt. I had the car towed and was told that I not only needed a transmission but a motor too.

Fuck that shit. I wasn't paying another dime to Jeff's girlfriend. I was the one wronged. I was a single parent and working minimum wage while his girlfriend worked at McDonald Douglas and Jeff worked at the school district. His girlfriend had hiring and firing power and wouldn't even get me in. I had an Associate's degree in Accounting. I would be able to hold my own once I got a position and I didn't understand why she didn't help a sister out.

Whatever!

I got my first credit card and was able to pay to get the Bug fixed.

I started dating a guy at the job named Anthony. Someone that

Charles took a liking to. We had fun and I was attracted to his dark skin. He was slim, tall and clean cut. We talked about moving in together and I thought of Candace. Was she ready to have a man in her life that was not her father? I know what I went through as a child and I didn't want her to go through that. I needed more time and then I had to test drive the merchandise. I had seen it through his pants but I had no idea that a penis could ever be that big. He was hung like a horse, no I mean literally. I was not able to take his full shaft. My hand between our bodies often buffered him going in too far and I still walked like I had something wedged in my special place days after intercourse. Candace liked him and I felt comfortable that he would never do anything to her. I made sure. I would tell him how I was her protector and murder was not out of the question when it came to

Candace.

I moved in with a man, whom I knew nothing about but what he told me. Charles had given us furniture and we went shopping for the rest of the necessities for our new apartment. In the beginning, everything was fine, but when I received a mysterious phone call from his mother that I had never met, he began to act strange.

She was trying to tell me something, but Anthony snatched the phone before she could tell me. All kind of alarms went off in my head. He became secretive and distant. I allowed him time to process whatever was bothering him, thinking he would come to me when he was ready but the unthinkable happened. He involved my child in the madness. One morning while we were getting dressed for work and Candace was watching her cartoons, he came and changed the channel to the news. I explained that she was already dressed then I changed the channel back to the cartoons and it became a channel switching struggle. I thought enough of this bull shit. I had endured the silent treatment and sleeping on the sofa and the distant behavior but once he started to affect Candace I was through. I changed the channel again and he pulled the plug out of the wall and I socked him in his jaw. As he staggered back, I was on top of him with the look of warning. He grabbed me and I pushed him off of me and socked him again. Candace just watched while he grabbed his jacket and walked out the door. He got a ride to work with Charles who lived in the same complex. I then drove Candace to her daycare center and went to work.

While at work I got the same silent treatment. He spoke to Charles and Sue but not a word was spoken to me. It was lunch time and Charles and Sue always ate alone. It was their special time and I admired that. I tried to talk to Anthony while I was putting out our lunch to eat and he began to walk away from me. I told him that we need to discuss what happened at home and he continued to walk away. I grabbed a can of soda and hit him square in him back. I felt bad and I wondered why I was trying to work on a dead relationship and we had only been living together for a month. All I wanted was a healthy relationship but that was not to be.

Chapter 16

Deidra had come back to California and I needed to talk to someone. I went to my boss and told him that I wasn't feeling well and I didn't. Tears filled my eyes at the thought of what I had done to Anthony. I was sad, hurt and I felt lost. My boss told me I could leave and I went home and called my sister. Deidra told me to come and see her in Montclair and I did after picking Candace up. When I got there I was a mess. What was I doing? Why nothing went as planned? I was frustrated and confused and all I wanted was peace. Deidra offered me a place with her and I accepted. I told her that I made a mistake in moving with this man that I knew nothing about and I felt that he was hiding something and I didn't want Candace to have any part of it. I went back to Southgate where the apartment was and packed our clothes. I called my job and told my boss that I quit and that was that.

Living with Deidra was better maybe because it was in California. I would be with my sisters and maybe they would finally see me for who I was. I needed them, wanting to have that sisterly bond that I had seen on television. We would cook together and she often wanted to hear about the things that I had been through in my twenty three years of living. Melanie also lived in the complex and would come over. I thought they were glad to have me there, but I later found out that wasn't the case.

I would take Candace out to dinner once a week to have some time alone. We would dress up in our best clothes and go dine. That became a problem for Deidra because she claimed that I should have told her so she wouldn't have cooked so much food. Although I apologized, it didn't make it right. My two sisters were beginning to gang up on me.

One night Melanie, Daddy Clyde, Deidre, and her husband and I were watching a movie that Daddy Clyde picked out. The movie was full of nudity and I began to feel uncomfortable.

Daddy Clyde began to make moaning sounds and commenting on how big the actress's breasts were. I had 38 triple D's and my sisters were mere B cups. He would often look at me which made memories of when I was ten. I began to feel like lunch and decided to excuse myself. Melanie jumped up and started screaming at me saying I thought I was too good to be in their company. I told them that I felt uncomfortable and that I preferred not to watch the movie and went into my room. I heard Deidre trying to calm Melanie down, but that was not my problem. I started listening to music to drown out the noise. Melanie knew what she had in that man and I was not going to subject myself to his vulgarity to please her.

The next morning, Deidra came to my room and told me I had thirty days to find somewhere else to live. I was in shock. What did I do? I asked and she stated that we just have different ways of living and are not compatible. I accepted the truth and set out to look for a job. I did get one at a famous toy store and was eager to share the good news. Deidra was not impressed.

Candace was now in kindergarten and I needed Deidra to pick her up from school when she went to get her son and Melanie's daughter. I told her I would pay her but she refused. I had to rely on friends that I had met while living with Deidra which was where I spent my time at home. I wanted to stay out of Deidra's way since the sight of me got her angry. I would have to leave my job on my lunch to get Candace from school then rush her to the sitter and hurry back to work. My sister would be parked behind me waiting for my niece and nephew. I was so hurt but I refused to show the pain. I acted like everything was alright.

The thirty days was fast approaching and I needed more time. I had saved enough money but I didn't have a place yet even though Candace and I searched and searched every chance we got. I went to Deidra and she wouldn't budge. I didn't want to rent a motel because then I wouldn't have the money needed to secured a permanent place so I humbled myself and asked Melanie if I could stay at her apartment for a few days. I would cook and clean whenever I wasn't working. Day after day Deidra would be parked behind me while I used my lunch time to take Candace to a friend. What was her problem with me? I didn't know but I refused to let her break me.

God intervened and I got the beautiful apartment in Ontario which was the next city from Montclair. The manager told me that her car was acting up and she had to come back home and there I was waiting for her. She said I was meant to have the apartment and told me it was mine. I was praising God. Candace and I would not be homeless. Our new home was in Ontario California and I moved in without a hitch and I continued to work and get a supplement from welfare. I was hired for seasonal for Christmas and I worked hard but I was given a pink slip after being told by the manager that I would get permanent status.

I wish that people could tell the truth. Didn't they know that I needed a job too? I had bills just like they did. I knew that God would provide and just went on my way.

It was Saturday. Jeff and his girlfriend came to visit. We were playing Dominos which was always a favorite in my family. It had turned into a big get together and soon Kevin and Jennifer were there and of course Melanie and her husband were there. We started talking about my father and Kevin and I listened intently because they were older and had more to tell. I felt this was a chance to learn more about my father when Deidra looked at me and said that she didn't think that daddy was my father and that Henry was my father. I asked her if she really thought mom had had an affair on my dad and she replied it wouldn't be the first. I was appalled and ready to knock the shit out of her. That was my mama and....

Hold up, did she just disown me? I wasn't her sister. I was half and the half she didn't like. I got Candace and left while the rest said nothing. I was alone.

I went home and called my mother who assured me that Henry was not my father but did I really care. I knew I was different. I refused to be ghetto, I carried myself with pride even though I was constantly criticized. My nose was too wide, and I was fat, now I'm not my daddy's child.

I'm still standing!

Now I understood why most of my siblings

were the way they were. They would put me down to build themselves up. They often criticized my actions even when I did the right thing. I quit trying to make them love me and considered myself alone and that was fine by me, it beats being bullied and mistreated.

Melanie and Deidra came over to my place to see how I was doing and I was leery of the motive. After the latest knife in my back, I guess I was skeptical of the visit.

My apartment was furnished with second hand furniture but it was nice. Deidra commented on the way I always land on my feet . I thought *God will always provide*, but I dare not say it out loud because of the debate that would ensue over my salvation. They had come by unexpected and I needed to go to the store and they went with me. At the register, a lady commented that she knew we were sisters because we looked so much alike. Melanie took me to the side and told me that applications were being accepted for Section 8 which is assistance for low income rent. She did it in such a way like she didn't want Deidra to know that she was trying to help me. I thanked her and got a newspaper which contained the application.

I was still socializing with the people I had met in Montclair and was introduced to crack cocaine. At first I was scared but I rationalized that it was recreational and it didn't harm one of the ladies that I knew. She was employed with L.A county and maintained her position, so I tried it. At first it felt good. I had not a care in the world. So what, I didn't have a job. I also didn't have any money so the experience would turn out to be short lived. They also taught me how to apply for credit cards and then laughed at me when I paid the bill. I figured that this was a wild bunch and soon distanced myself from them. I knew I had issues and didn't need anymore.

I was only in the apartment for about two months when I received a letter notifying me of a interview for Section 8. I was later accepted and had to move because my complex didn't participate in the program. I got a list and began my quest for another place. I went east and found a place in Fontana California which was fine by me. I didn't have anything keeping me in Los Angeles and I didn't want to raise Candace there. I quickly enrolled back in school to work on transfer units to get to Cal State University San Bernardino. I took speech, Philosophy and English 102 and did well at the classes. I would work at the hardware store in the summer to give my mother a break, but I needed the money because I soon gave Crack a try.

The monkey that I had eluded was back with a vengeance. I would call myself a weekend closet smoker. Only a party of two and no more than when the greed of my fellow crackheads thought they were getting over on me hogging what I had purchased, I let them go. I remember a time when I was smoking with this guy name Thomas. He used to be my standby. My booty buddy, my companion without strings, my friend with benefits. There was no pretense and it was good for us both. He did have a girlfriend but I gave her respect even though he didn't. I often saw bruises on her face when she came by to visit him. This nigga was a beater; I wish he would. I told him that I was a victim of domestic violence and how it made me feel. I don't know if I told him that as a warning not to try or to tell him what his girlfriend may be feeling. He tried to force me to have sex with him. I guess he thought I was on the losing end on the domestic violence event in my life until I threw him across the room and over a sofa. After he got his bearings about himself, he tried to say he was just playing. I told him not to ever play with me that way. So many emotions came up in me and even though I was high, I wouldn't allow myself to become a victim. I could have killed him. I thought about the many times that men tried to take what I was not willing to give. I left and never smoked, dated or fucked him again. I still would speak to him but the thrill was gone. I became a lone smoker and I would go all the way to the projects off of Alameda and Imperial to buy drugs. I was a good mother in the daytime then when I put Candace to bed I would wait until she was sleep then I would lose my mind. I left her home along to go cop drugs then I would come back home to smoke it. Sometimes I would do it three or four times in a night. One twenty dollar rock would often turn into eighty dollars a night on the weekend. I had lost control of what I rationalized as recreational. I was lost and needed help. I had gone too far and didn't know how to get back.

I wanted to quit so bad that I thought if I confessed it I would stop, but that only gave people the ammunition to talk about me. I did; however get along better with my siblings. My nephew used to sell it and I tried to cop from him and he refused me. I couldn't be mad at him because he made me feel ashamed.

I was his aunt and instead of trying to tell him the dangers of drug selling or using I was trying to get a rock. I realized how low I had sunk and that I didn't like what I had become. I was propositioned by a drug dealer to be his girlfriend and I told him just to give me the drugs that I pay for. I was in enough trouble being an addict, I didn't want to be dependent too. All the time I had copped I had a guardian angel covering my dumb behind. I once copped at a project in South Central and soon after getting the drugs in my hand and getting into my car I was surrounded by unmarked police cars. They ordered me out of the car and took my purse. I had put the rock under my seat cover and they never found it. I made an excuse for being in the neighborhood at 1o'clock in the morning. I was released and instead of quitting I went home and smoked that rock shaking as I did it. I broke many pipes only to purchase new ones. I knew I was spiraling out of control but I had not a clue of what to do or who to talk to. I would see commercials about drugs on television only to get a craving to go cop. I would get diarrhea and dry mouth. I was a crack head. Once I smoked a joint with Jerry and Marie called primo. I was sitting on the floor when I hit the joint and after a couple of puff, puff passes I fell back on the floor and was paralyzed. I could hear everything, but I couldn't move. Jerry and Marie thought I was asleep, but I wasn't. They started to talk about personal issues and I mustered enough strength to speak telling them that I was not sleep and if they were to not talk about anything they want to remain between them. I slept with a neighbor of Jerry's that still lived with his mama. A real loser that didn't have a job. I would later be reminded of by Jerry wanting to prove how out of control I was. I could do nothing but agree with everything that Jerry said because it was true. I felt that God was speaking to me. In my foolishness, he had something for me to do. I finally fell to my knees one day after Candace came to me complaining that her finger was hurting. One look at the nail and I began to cry. She assured me that it didn't hurt as bad as that, but I was emotional because I felt that I had let her down. Her nail was about to fall off and I was just now seeing it. I felt neglectful. That night I prepared Candace dinner and gave her a bath then tucked her into bed. I went to my room and I prayed to God for forgiveness and to save me from this life that I created for myself. I praised him and thanked him. I begged for forgiveness until I began to speak in another tongue. I was grieved but yet shocked that I no longer had control of my tongue. In my mind I saw family members and situations as the tongues changed. I don't know how long I was praying but I was exhausted when I was finished. I went to wash my face and it was beet red. I felt different but didn't know what to make of it until I woke up the next morning and saw the commercial about this is your brain on crack and nothing happened. No dry mouth, no diarrhea, I started to praise the Lord for delivering me and I promised that I would never take an illegal drug ever again. I began to pray and look at the course of my life. Everything that I was ashamed of, I repented and asked God to forgive me. I cried over the abortions and the lives of the babies lost. I promised never to have another abortion.

I began to change.

Chapter 17

Suddenly I saw life differently. I wanted to please God because I was grateful for his grace and mercy. I knew I was the one he died for and I had a purpose not yet revealed to me. It was 1989, the year I was told by God that I was the special one. I often wondered why I was compelled to record on my greeting that I was the special one. I knew I was supposed to do something but I didn't know what. I was attending Cal State San Bernardino and felt that I was not fully committed to my education and I wanted to get away from the memories of the drug years.

A longtime friend from high school, Debra Stevens, came to visit me and convinced me to move to El Centro, CA where she now lived with her husband and children. I left a life I wanted to forget and entered into another life of alcohol and late night bar hopping. I tried talking to my friend about her behavior and that I didn't understand why she was so loose. She explained that she was going to do what she wanted without limits. In my mind, I thought I did have limits because I knew what I had come out of.

I got a job as an account clerk and smoked cigarettes like a train. This was the first job that I had and I felt out of place. I worried if I was completing the forms correctly and took it hard when I made mistakes. I apologized for the least little thing. I had an uneasy feeling about my living situation and it was confirmed when Debra and her husband propositioned me for a threesome. I was in shock. The thoughts that went on in my head about burning in hell and defiling the marital bed ran through my mind. How could they ask me such a thing? They always called me Miss Goody-Two-Shoes and now they had nerve to wonder why I declined. At that point my comfort level went to zero and I realized I had made a big mistake.

One day after a lot of thought I decided it was time to return to San Bernardino and deal with the monkeys that I was afraid to face. I failed at school, I had no work experience other than warehouse jobs and I was now homeless.

What the fuck!

Life was supposed to be easier when I grew up but instead it was more difficult. I went back to the Welfare office and applied for assistance again. A scene all too familiar. Depression everywhere I looked and workers who tried to put you down with every question. I was humbled and needed the help, so I endured the disrespect for the help that was going to get Candace and I off the streets. I drove to my sister, Melanie's house, and told her what was happening. I told her that I was no longer on drugs and that I made a mistake by moving and letting my Section 8 go. I asked her if I could live with her until I got back on my feet. She spoke to Daddy Clyde who said it would not be a good idea and I was disappointed but I understood until they allowed Jake and his girlfriend to move in with them. Candace and I lived in a motel in San Bernardino with the help of Homeless assistance. God intervened and I was approved for Section 8 again. I was grateful.

I quickly found a place and found a temp job for the Harris Co. I thought of my grandfather and his evilness but praised God for the job and realized that he had saved me from his advances. There I met a girl name Sandra. She was a nice person but she had issues but who was I to judge. She was married and had a nice family, two boys and a daughter. Her husband was a military man and I felt happy for her but sad for myself. I wanted to be married and have a house but I felt that because of the life I had led that it was not in my cards. Sandra and I quickly formed a bond of friendship and I felt that this was the sister that I always wanted. We talked all the time and I did a lot of things with her family. I was glad to have someone to be close to. I had Candace, but I needed someone that I could talk to; I needed to get all my feelings out. The things that bothered me and fears that I had not yet dealt with. I was a single parent on welfare working a temp job with an associate's degree. I know it had to be more to my life and I felt stuck. I was lonely and felt that if I only had a boyfriend, a companion I would be fine. I would go out with Sandra and often wondered why she was out there. She had what I wanted; a man that loved her even though she has an indiscretion that produced a biracial child and he still stayed. I didn't understand her way of thinking. What was she looking for out there? I would sit at the bar drinking my Long Island Ice Tea watching people on the dance floor and would not dare do the things they were doing. I was a saved individual in this booty call den named TOPS in San Bernardino. The night often ended with sore feet and not so much as a glance in my direction. So much for my self-esteem. I refused to show my assets to get attention. I always covered my 42 Triple D's and my booty was always hidden, but guys would still look at my breast when they spoke to me. I would have to redirect their eyes to my face. Candace was now ten and getting sneakier. I often told her that God blessed me to know her and that she was not getting away with anything. She would wait until I was ill and act out in the worst way. Junior was nonexistent and I had to deal with the many issues that came up and there were many. Stealing at the corner convenient store, hanging out with the bad kids in the complex and trying to talk back to me. I don't think so. One time Candace wanted to go outside and play with the other misguided youth and I told it was not a good idea because and I was not feeling well. She took off running out the front door. I ran after her and realized I was not dressed. Sure I had pajamas on without a bra and all my assets were all over the place. I was dizzy, weak and I was angry as hell that she chose this moment to pull this shit. She ran right pass a parked police car who did nothing. This was the hood and this kind of stuff happened all the time around here. I was reduced to a statistic, Bebe and her kid. I returned to my apartment crying and ready to give up. I called my mother who told me to let her go. Candace was a ten year old child and I was not going to let her go like I felt my mother did to me. This madness had to stop and it was going to stop with me. I looked out the window and saw Candace walking up the stairs at another building in the complex. I interrupted my mother and the nonsense that she was speaking. I got dressed and put on my running shoes and I was determined to go and get my baby. The streets couldn't have her. I had authority over her no just by law but by God.

I went to the apartment and Candace was shocked that I had found her. She ran into the kitchen and picked up a rusty butcher knife. She pointed it at me and told me to stay back and that she was warning me.

Oh this heifer had seen too many movies. I moved closer to her and grabbed the knife wielding hand and punched her in her stomach. How dare this little kid, MY CHILD, ever threaten me with a knife? I told her to get up and she refused and I told her to have it her way and proceeded to drag her by her braids that I so neatly put in. After a couple of steps hitting that ass she decided that she had better get up. I held on to her hair and I walked her home while she pleaded for help from everyone we passed. I just kept walking. I got her home and tried to get her to talk to me about her behavior. I didn't know what would make her threaten me let along disobey me. I sat there trying to build up the courage to whoop that ass. I knew I couldn't let her get away with that kind of behavior even though I was sick as a dog. While I was talking to her I heard a loud knock on the door. It was the police and I thought oh now you want to get involved. I calmly went to the door and let them in. I sat while Candace talked about how I pulled her hair and socked her in her stomach. As she talked about abuse the officers looked around the apartment. They questioned me about the alleged abuse and I explained that she pulled a knife on me. The officer than directed the comment to Candace to her amazement that she was heading quickly towards juvenile delinquency. He told her that she lived in a nice place and that I had her best interest in mind. He told her if he was to come back it would be her he will take. He turned and apologized for the inconvenience and left and I felt that he just gave me license to exercise my parental rights and I commenced to whooping that ass. I then reverse the lock on her bedroom door and gave her some water and a pot to piss in. Good night!

The lock stayed that way until she came to me and told me that she knew she was wrong. I knew I didn't want to wake to a knife in my back and I was not going to be a victim not even to my daughter. I explained to her that if she ever threaten my life I would forget she was my child and I would defend myself till death if need be. Her facial expression let me knew that she understood what I was saying.

Junior showed up with his sorry ass looking like an out of date playboy. He was still wearing the clothes that he had when I was with him some eight years back. Somebody needed to tell him the polyester was out. Candace reacted like he was her knight coming to rescue her from the evil step mother while he was trying to determine if I was hot or cold. After taking Candace out he dropped her off and that was that. Fuck him. Who needs a sometime father? Not me. Someone also needed to tell him that fatherhood was not a part time position.

A month had pass since the last appearance from dear old dad and Candace started to act out again. Apparently, he had taken her up to his place in Big Bear and she concocted a plan to be with him. She ran away and told the police that I was abusive and that she didn't want to live with me anymore. I wasn't through. *Abusive.* I was good to that child and was often criticized by my family for giving her so much. Not monetary, but my time. Nothing came before Candace and this little girl lied and defamed my character all for a chance to stay with her father. I wasn't going to stand in her way. If she felt that she would be better off with him I would let her go. It came with some pain. I was depressed and alone. My daughter didn't even want me. What the hell was happening? I thought. That child didn't have any loyalty. Her friends were all jealous because of how good she had it including my family and she does this to me. Junior brought her back on the pretense that she was there to get her things and said he had to go to the car. It was a while and Candace and I were finish packing her belongings. I told her to go and get her father whom I assumed didn't want to be in the same room as me. Candace came back crying like someone just stole her heart. She was yelling and fretting. He was gone. After I quieted her, I asked, "Where did he lived?" I followed her directions which led me to a house on a cul de sac. I went to the door and I could hear moans and groans coming from a window. I told Candace to stay in the car. This no good bastard just abandoned his daughter and was now fucking a wildebeest from the sounds of it. That was some sick shit. It sounded like something from a porn movie and all that was not needed to have good sex. I thought, that motherfucker was kinky as hell. I realized his demons went far beyond my imagination.

I banged on the door like I was a cop and I had a hammer that I had pulled from the trunk of my car. He peeked out the window and I told him to bring his ass outside. I told him he was pathetic and I don't understand how he could do what he was doing. I told him I would not leave until he came out and told his daughter that he didn't want her or to take her. I knew his past and the child molestation conviction but I had to leave it to God because Candace was determined to have her way and that was with him. The hoochie came out in some dollar store lingerie looking like a hooker but that was his business.. My problem was not with her so I didn't talk about her bad. I told her what he did and she convinced him to go and get Candace's things. I got in my car and went back home. I prayed that I was doing the right thing. I didn't want Candace to be traumatized by this sicko she called daddy. I had to get myself together when they came to my apartment and to come to terms that I was letting my daughter go. Candace had changed into biker shorts which she knew I forbidden her from wearing but that was to show me that she could do what she wanted and that I was too strict. I said nothing about her attire and started moving her things to the door.

"Ooh mom, do you think I need to take this?" Candace said. I said "If you want it." She looked at me and said, "Oh no, not you." then turned to look at the hoochie.

Candace was trying to hurt me and she was cutting me deep. Her friend's mother was there and she held my hand and I refused to cry even though I was about to break down. My child had disowned me without a blink of her eye. What did I do but love this child? I thought of the many hours of labor the extra, weight gain, the Bells Palsy and all to be dissed by my own child. I was ready for her to leave. I just wanted the pain to end and she was my pain.

Life without Candace was empty. I couldn't think or eat. I called but got no answer. I had no idea of how she was. If she was happy. If she was okay. I could only pray that she was. A month had passed and I called the welfare and Section 8 office to tell them that she was no longer with me. I was going to lose my aid and had to get a smaller apartment for one. I was going to be forced to get out there and get a real job with benefits. The next day, Junior called stating that he had to bring Candace back. I told him to bring her home and immediately called the Department of Behavior health. I knew that she was going to need counseling. Her father was bringing her back to the one place she didn't want to be. With me. I didn't know when she was coming and I had no food in the house. I waited until the moron brought my daughter home and then I got a friend to take me shopping because I didn't have a car at the time. We were in the grocery store and she began throwing a tantrum, screaming and kicking the basket I told her that I knew she was hurting but she was not going to act like that. I tried to change the subject with a choice of cereal and I asked her about Sugar Frosted Flakes and the heifer told me that they taste better in Rancho Cucamonga. I was through. I grabbed her by her throat in the middle of the store and told her I had enough. I told her if she said one more disrespectful thing, I would snap her neck like a twig and I meant it. I didn't have to take her back. Child Protection took her to her father. She was in his custody and I took her back because I loved her and she was talking shit. My friend pulled me off of her and I went to the register.

When I got home I said nothing, I went to the kitchen and prepared dinner. Candace was in her room and didn't come out until I called her for dinner. We ate in silence and with the shit that I had heard come out of her mouth it was fine by me. I finished dinner and went to take my plate to the kitchen and when I turned to go to the living room, she was standing right in front of me. She hugged me and started to cry and I cried with her. I told her that I knew that the pain hurt, but I didn't deserve the treatment I was getting. I apologized for the incident in the store and that I truly loved her. We started counseling that next week and a lot of what I went through with her father was discussed. I never bad mouth her father, and she was shocked to hear all that I endured. It became a tradition that we would got out to dinner every Wednesday after therapy.

Chapter 18

The county of San Bernardino had called and offered me a job and the money was okay. Who am I kidding! The money was great. I had never made that much money and I was grateful. I took the test a while ago and I had an interview and was chosen for one of many positions. In training, all the trainees were talking about the position that they previous had and I felt like a loser. I had not managed anything in my life, and the only work I did was warehouse and I sat in the class with professional egg heads who were lying through their teeth. I decided to be honest and talk about my life and my testimonies. I told the truth about being on welfare and that this was my first office job.

I began to tell what God had done but I .didn't want to be spooky. I didn't know about the many books of the bible but I knew I believed. I knew that God gave his son so that we would have everlasting life. I went to church but found that I was not happy with church doctrine. I believed that you do unto other as you would have them do to you and the Ten Commandments. I would get offended by church goers who were mean spirited and wondered why they bothered to come to church. The word was good and the message was well received and still people would be backbiting right outside the church doors. I never involved myself with the auxiliaries because often my spirit would be wounded by what went on. I knew what God did for me and I was not going to waste it. I felt that life was getting better and I wanted to share it with someone and now I was gainfully employed.

I started dating this guy who lived in my

apartment complex. He looked like Billy Dee and had a swagger about him. I was a little green because I didn't know the nigga was a drunk. I knew what I was doing was wrong but I had needs and it had been a year since I had sex and I had to convince myself that I still had it.

You know. Sex appeal.

His name was Hosie, yes real name, from some back hoe down, south country town. I liked him and I began drinking and socializing with a different group of people. I felt unwanted and I didn't was to die a lonely old woman with nothing but heart ache so I took a chance and jumped in with both feet even though I knew it was not of God. Those damned monkeys. I was getting them from the media, the doctors, my family and my friends. You should do this; you should do that is what I heard constantly. I encouraged Hosie to find employment and helped him purchase and car. I was going to build a man if it was the last thing I did. What a joke. I couldn't build a man, but you couldn't tell me any different. I would buy him the things I wanted to see him in. The cologne I wanted to smell and create the atmosphere of romance but I was indeed fooling myself. I didn't get it until Candace came to me in her sleep. I heard her calling my name Mommy while she patted me softly. I asked her what was going on and she told me that Homie was no good. This shit was affecting my child and in her sleep. I cradled her and I felt like shit. My daughter knew more than me. I got to get rid of Homie alright.

That next day after work and before our usual Friday office happy hour, I went to get my key from Hosie who was staying with his friend.

His friend's wife led me to where he was sleeping and I notice all the female things that was in the room along with his stuff. I laid on the bed then shook him and nearly scared to shit out of him. He started to look around to see how busted he was and he was pretty caught. I laid in another woman's bed and he was trying to get me off the bed. The wife's sister's bed and I didn't care. She knew what she was doing when she brought me back here. I spoke better and I was educated but I was still street. That day, I was ready to jump into somebody's ass. I was tired of getting screwed over. What did I do to deserve this disrespect? I couldn't even make a nigga. With his dumb ass. So why not break a nigga. I politely asked for my key and he asked me why. I told him to look around and that he didn't deserve my key. I told him, that Candace called him Homie and that I didn't like the way that the relationship or lack thereof was affecting my daughter and then he called me a bitch, that his name was not Homie. There were only three things that would make me throw the first punch. Calling me a bitch was one of them. The other two: don't fuck with my kid or my money. I had just got played by this loser country bumpkin. I socked him in the jaw and he pushed me out of my stilettos that I had worn for happy hour. I went down in a sweeping motion and grabbed one of the shoes and turn and grabbed that nigga by his wife beater and ripped it off of his back before I embedded my heel into his back. His friend came and pulled me off of him and took me outside. I told him he will think twice before he screw over a woman and laugh.

I went to happy hour as usual and had a

drink when one of my coworkers noticed that I had blood on my face. That punk ass nigga scratched like the bitch he was. I dismissed the subject as I wiped the blood from my face and took another drink of my Ice Tea. I sat there feeling conviction for what I had done. I knew better and I knew I could not tell anyone that I was a child of God. I was too ashamed. My behavior was not a good witness to the good news that Jesus saves. After I got home I fell on my face for the way I was acting. The conviction was too great. I saw where I was a year ago and knew that it was God grace and mercy that brought from drug addiction. I repented and then found out I was pregnant. How could this have happened? I used birth control responsibly and I still got pregnant. I remember the promise I made to God and I realized that I was not going to have an abortion. I was going to have a baby and this time with a guy who had no aspirations and no intelligence and didn't keep a job long enough to pay child support.

This time the monkey was causing a huge speed bump and I could do nothing but accept it. I prayed about my situation and honored my vow. I told my mother that I was expecting and she was not pleased but didn't say anything bad about it. I loved her for that, I didn't need to hear what I was already saying to myself that I had messed up and was putting more difficulty in an already hard life. I had gotten used to thinking of having a baby when I started to bleed. I called my doctor and told her what was happening and she told me to stay off my feet and I did until I had to use the bathroom and then I lost it. There was no pain, no excessive bleeding but I felt loss. I grieved for about a week and then went back to work. I believe that because of the previous abortion, it was punishment and the guilt monkey consumed me. I later moved on and decided that I needed to stay out of relationships for a while. I concentrated on work, church and got involve with the church I was attending and found it to be some evil people in the church.

My family started to turn from me not just leave me alone but start rumors. Something was always wrong with me. *She doesn't come around, I think she is still on drugs, or she's a snob.* I knew now who to go to for all my worries and I didn't need the approval of my family. I was blessed and highly favored and it showed in my confidence which people took for arrogance. I couldn't win for losing and I got whiplash from all the cheek turning so I moved further away. I kept in touch, I just became guarded. I loved my life and Candace and I were finally doing okay. I remained listed with the telephone company so the moron Eagle Scout could find her when we moved to Summerwind, a nice condominium, in Highland I no longer needed Section 8 but I appreciated all that the program gave to me in the form of reduced rent. One day, Candace and I were walking the track near our home and we heard a familiar voice and Candace took off running to the gate. It was her father playing basketball at the school on the corner. I was shocked to see him but he looked embarrass to see us. He came to the gate and told my eleven year old baby to consider him dead. I grabbed Candace and held her tight. That bastard. Why was he so mean? Why was he trying to destroy my child? I talked about him so bad in front of the guys he was playing with that he left the court. Candace and I resumed our walk. I talked about the therapy and that we could not let the idiot ruin our progress and she agreed. I called all the feelings that hurt us monkeys. The low self-esteem, fear, doubt, even a waste of money was a monkey.

I was on a journey of self-discovery and completely unaware of my transformation. All I knew was that I was growing and things that mattered before didn't matter now. Happy hour was a thing of the past, although I didn't stop drinking entirely. I became a social drinker for special occasions and then it was only wine. I would only depend on God for my provisions and needed no one. I would discuss matters of importance and gave people the opportunity to be a blessing, but I would not beg. I also would be a blessing to others. When I saw a need, I was there to assist without strings. I tried to be more like Jesus and help as help was needed. I bought Candace a bracelet WWJD (What would Jesus do). I prayed for a husband, but I would not flirt. I became demure and I was happy and at peace. My job was not far from my home, however, it was not walking distance. I began catching the bus to work and refused a ride because I wanted to truly appreciate a vehicle when the Lord blessed me with one. I bought a grocery basket to shop and Candace and I went to the store every weekend. It was a humbling experience and I prayed for the time to get transportation. I saved my money and a friend went with me to a car dealer and I purchased my first new car. It was a black Ford Escort. I remember rolling down the street praising God for the blessing. No more buses, no more baskets. I paid the price for humility and God blessed me with

Black Beauty.

It was now 1992 and Candace and I had a quiet evening at home and the doorbell rang. It was Junior. I invited him in and he came to apologize for the dead comment. I told him that he needed to direct that at Candace because she was mostly affected by it. He took her shopping and when they returned, I spoke to him about braces for her teeth.

At the time he was paying $100 a month and I asked for an additional $44. He said that he paid child support and that was all he was obligated to pay and I said not another word. I went inside and wrote a letter to the district attorney requesting that the order be modified. It took six months but the child support increased to $562 a month. The last thing I said in court was that you pay child support and that is all you're obligated to pay and left. I felt strong and confident and the Lord directed my path and I liked the feeling.

Chapter 19

My friend Cher and I was close. I met her at work and we quickly became friends. She was the one that took me to purchase my first car. I liked her a lot and treated her like the little sister I never had. We would go out together and she was going through a bitter break up with her husband. I tried to encourage and be there when she needed an ear. I had

never been married but I knew the lost of a relationship. We worked for the County of San Bernardino and had pool parties and girls night out. Sandra didn't like Cher but she had a few monkeys of her own to deal with. The closer Cher and I got the further Sandra and I became till we barely spoke. I guess I didn't miss her that much because I was the giver in the relationship and she always had a need even with a husband; she was just greedy.

Cher and I would shop, watch movies, go to clubs featuring male exotic dancers, and attend concerts.

We started working out to get my weight down. I was over 250 pounds and stood five feet five inches tall. I had a body it was just a big body. I lost forty pounds and I felt fabulous. Cher stood five eight with caramel skin and long pretty hair. She weighed about one thirty and had a look of Pocahontas. She had the look but I had the self-esteem and the angry. I refused to let a man tell me that I was not worthy. Cher on the hand had a bad relationship with her husband. I think he was abusive, but Cher never discussed it and I never push the issue. I would share about my

abuse to give her the assurance that I understood what she may have been
going through, but she never opened up, verbally that is.

Cher had a voice that sound like Mary J Blige and the look to sell albums but her confidence was in the toilet. I encouraged her to sing in her sister's band. We went to see her sister perform at Boomers at the Raddison hotel. That's where I first saw the guy that would one day be my a husband.

He was dark skinned and average weight but a little on the short side. He stood about an inch shorter than me. He had a look of Teddy Pendergrass, Veen Bereen, and Scotty from the Whispers.

The performance was great and when Shaka sang "At Last" I was amazed. That girl could blow. She had the crowd eating out of her hands and I was in that crowd. She later introduced me as her hair stylist because I would weave her hair to give her the Chaka Khan look. As I stood to the intro, I noticed that the keyboardist was watching. At the time I had put it out of my mind because I was on a diet from men since Hosie. It had been going on three years and I was fine. I would go to the rehearsals with Cher for support. Candace was old enough to be at home alone and I was not out too long for her to get into anything and she also knew I didn't play.

One night at rehearsal, we were locked out because no one had the key and Cher, Nate (my future), this bass player named Jerry and myself was talking about peanut butter and jelly sandwiches. Don't ask me why but I just said, "…and a cold glass of milk." We all started to

laugh and
that's when I saw that smile. His teeth were perfect.

We finally got into the room to start rehearsal and I sat to encourage Cher and to build that confidence. As the guys set up, Cher and I sat while I smoked a cigarette. I knew she didn't like it so I made sure the smoke never went in her direction.

I would give her encouraging words to assure her that she would be fine. As she took the mic, I knew she was nervous so I told her to breathe. She smiled and then she opened her mouth and the words came out. At first they were a little smothered and I motioned for her to let it go and that's when she let go and showed out. I almost fell out of my chair. I believed her when she said she could sing but I didn't know she had it like that. She sang "Love Without a limit" by Mary J. Blige and it was ready to record. As I listened in amazement I felt that someone was staring at me and when I looked at Nate he put his head down. This happened a couple of times more than I just kept staring at him and when he decided to take another look, I was already looking dead in his face. He was so embarrassed that he lost where he was and had to caught up. I began to laugh. At the end of rehearsal we left and that was that until the next rehearsals.

After several rehearsals, Cher was ready to perform and she was great. All eyes were on her and I was so proud like a big sister. This was also the first time Cher met Alex. She was taken with him. He was nice but I knew he was a user, a parasite, and Cher was the host. I tried talking to her about guarding herself and to not let the night life consume her. She assured me that she had it covered. He also performed at the club and he was good. He had the ladies drooling and Cher was secretly impressed. I kept my legs under the table because I didn't want any man between my legs.

Nate needed a ride at the closing of the club and I volunteered to take him home. Him and all his baggage, keyboards, amp and stand. Damn, I thought I was going to drop him off and it turned out to be a moving job in heels no less. We talked all the way to his place and then in the car. I was amazed the he knew the Lord and he started talking about his dreams and they were my dreams. He was a man, with dreams and I was a woman who wanted to go along for the ride. I was comfortable with him and I was not looking at him in that way as yet, but it made sense to me. We briefly talked about our mothers who shared the same name and was born in the same month. I thought, Lord, is my praying being answered. I was still leery and after four hours of talking, I told him it was time that I went to Cher's house to get Candace who was watching Cher's two children. He asked if he could have a kiss and I told him that if I had to think about it I guessed not. Nate respected my decision and I left. On the drive to get Candace, I thought this man didn't try to get me into his apartment or try to get me to take him to mine. That was impressive, since sex in that day was to be conquered. I felt safe.

I hadn't talked to Nate until another performance at the club and then we exchanged numbers. I think that I began to pursue him. Every time I would call, he would say I was about to call you. Yeah right.

One time he said it and I asked what was my number and he went silent. I laughed and told him that if I was calling too much and if I made him feel uncomfortable I would not call again and he begged me not to. I later found out that he was shy as they come.

Our first date was on October 30, 1993. We went to the Redondo Beach Pier and had dinner a Tony's. The lobster and the clam chowder was great. Nate had never went on a date like this and I always had dreams of how I wanted to be treated. He paid for everything but I had money of my own. We walked the pier, looked at rings in a shop, for which he tried to buy me one and I told him that I will not put a ring on until I have thee ring. We also went to listen to a Reggae band in one of the bars. I was singing to him and then I kissed him. I think we both

were stunned because we watched as the wine glass tipped over, rolled off the table and shatter on the floor. That woke us up and I could see

that Nate was uncomfortable and embarrassed so I jokingly said that I never had a guy break a glass for me. We apologized to the waiter who said no problem, then we left. I had planned the evening and I didn't know what Nate's finances were, but I wanted to have a good time. I offered to pay and he said that a lady doesn't pay when she is with him.

Ooh goose bumps.

As we walked back to the car I started to sing, even though I couldn't carry a tune, Sam Cooke's tune, A Change is Going To Come and he finished it. I told him that I didn't know he could sing and he told me that when he marries me he will write me a song. I was on cloud nine. This man was nice and he wasn't all thugged out. He was a gentleman even with his touch. It was almost like he could sense my past and the hurt that I had encountered.

From the Beach we ended our night at the Comedy Store on Sunset Blvd. Nate was from New Orleans and I wanted to show him the city. The only place he knew was San Bernardino and Norton Air force base.

We got back to my place around two in the morning. We were still hyped from the day's events and were not ready for the night to end and it didn't. When I got inside, I hit the switch to turn on the fireplace to set the mood. I didn't know what was in his mind but burning fire was all up in my loins. My breast were sensitive to the touch. I quivered with anticipation. My breathing was deep and heavy as I felt the budge in his pants as we kissed. He wasn't a good kisser, but we had all the time to practice. I could tell that Nate was not experience because he was very nervous, but he quickly got in the mood. The clothes were flying everywhere until were both fell on the sofa laughing. I felt comfortable and I had not had sex in three years. I was long overdue and the excitement was driving me crazy. We got busy right there on the sofa because Candace was at a friend's house and we had total privacy. Once he entered, I felt that we were a good fit. My walls were tight around his shaft and I concentrated on every move. I didn't want it to end, but I couldn't hold on. Then it happened, we both exploded in ecstasy with sweat dripping from his face. At last, a man willing to work. Hot dog!

We finally move to the bedroom where we took a bath together and laid in each other's arms. I was like a kid in a candy store, a Christian coming off a fast, a teenager on Christmas day. It was now time to begin again and Nate was willing. We moved to the bed and went at it again and again it until we both collapsed and sleep fell on the both of us.

Chapter 20

We spent every weekend together and Candace didn't mind. I was at every performance that he had. We were inseparable. I felt like I was a teenager with a high school crush. Although Candace and Nate had never met, she knew that I was happy and that the leash that I had on her was finally loosened. Nate and Candace both wanted to meet each other and I was not sure it was the right time. I prayed for forgiveness for fornicating but my flesh was weak. I knew right and all I could do was pray for grace and mercy. Two weeks had pass and after much nagging from both Candace and Nate, I invited him to dinner. I made Lasagna, salad and garlic bread. Oh yeah! I am a good cook.

At first they just stared at each other and then we sat down to dinner to break the ice. Candace started the conversation and Nate was impressed with how well she spoke. He was on every word and she liked the attention. She never had a man in her life and she was comfortable with Nate and so was I.

After dinner, Candace dismissed herself and went to her room.

She gave me the thumbs up before leaving. I was glad she liked him.

Nate and I sat and talked while listening to old school music.

I spent less time with Cher and I think that put a strain on our relationship. She in turned spent more time with Alex who was not a keeper. He would often disrespect her and one night made the mistake of talking shit to her in my presence. I jumped out of her brand new Camaro and asked her why she was letting him talk to her like that. I was ready to kick his ass and he knew I was not afraid. We left the club and I was pissed. I told her she could do better and she didn't. She just replaced the dancer for another low life dancer.

On Thanksgiving, I took Nate to meet my family and introduced him as my fiancé. My family was shocked because they said I was too mean to get married. I was just too honest. My mother said Nate must be a real man or he was just plain stupid. I assured her that he was a real man, a Christian man, a gentleman and left it at that. Charles was not so excited. He told me not to marry him because he was too dark and people that dark were evil. I knew what I felt and felt that God had given me my desire, a husband who Candace and I felt safe with.

Nate started going to my bowling tournaments and he kept Candace company, bowling with her on a different lane. We spent all of our free time together and I enjoyed every minute.

One evening I went to get Nate because he didn't have a car. During our time together he told me that he was going to New Orleans for Christmas and I was crushed until he told me that he wanted to take Candace and me along. I was surprised and excited. I talked to Candace and she was okay with the trip, so we started making plans. Her birthday was coming up and I planned to take her bowling. Her father decided to show up for her birthday and I told him that we will be going bowling and he agreed to meet us there. He showed up wearing tight jeans and one of his lame shiny black shirts.

He wore sun glasses even at night which made him look stupid as hell but what did I care. He had Candace's present in hand and he notice upon approach that we weren't alone. I saw his body tense up as he got closer and I was tickled inside. I guess he wondering if I was going to be hot or cold and he got the answer. I introduced Nate as my fiancé and his jaw dropped. They shook hands and I went to bowl so Junior couldn't see my face. The satisfaction was too much for me to contain and it would have be rude to laugh at the man in his face. Junior didn't stay long and Candace didn't mind. She was happy and Nate gave her the attention and the daddy time that she needed.

I took two weeks off from work and we drove to New Orleans. All I had to say was that Texas was big. I thought New Orleans was swampy but it was metropolitan. It was a nice city and the weather was great. I met his mother and siblings and they seemed to be nice. She allowed us to share the same room since we were already living together and I didn't see anything wrong with it but it was. It was disrespectful and I knew better, but the monkey on my back was too great. We ate good food and went shopping and stayed up late drinking. My liquor of choice was Tequila shots while his mother drank beer through a straw. During our visit, Nate and I got sick and his mother made me a hot toddy. I was well for Christmas while Nate who did not drink hard liquor refused the tonic and was sick. We went bowling and I whooped his brothers butts and they were shock that they got beat by a woman. We took many pictures at the Audubon Zoo when we took Candace and his two nieces. We rode the ferry and visited the river walk.

Nate and I left Candace with her soon to be cousins and went to to the House of Blues where Angela Bofield performed. We had a ball and that was the first vacation that I had ever taken. I met a lot of his family, aunts, uncles, cousins, nieces and nephews.

This is what Candace needed. I wanted to give her a family and the experience of an active grandmother. They were close knit and New Orleans would be a great place to visit again.

We returned home and started thinking of plans for the wedding. My mind was made up and Nate was the man for me. We planned for a July wedding but after attending church and several repentant prayers

Nate told me that we had to get married right away. I made a joke and asked him if he was pregnant, but I could see it wasn't funny. He told me he couldn't take the quilt of living in sin and I was actually relieved because I knew that we were wrong. We both believed that God put us together then we showed our gratitude by living in sin. We were abusing grace and mercy and the conviction was too great for Nate. Cher helped me plan a wedding and a bridal shower in five days, that girl had skills, which is why she was my maid of honor.

The bridal shower was great with a male exotic dancer that I knew. He was no stranger and I felt comfortable with him and since the ladies wanted one I went with the Candy licker. He showed us a good time and I was prepared with two maxi pads and a one piece outfit so none of my asset could be exposed. Cher did the same thing but the other four ladies were fair game. The candy licker licked toes and went under blouses and unzipped a few pants but Cher and I were safe. Thank God for thinking ahead.

The wedding was at the Hall of Records and Cher and a few friends helped out with decorations and it was nice. Nate did write me a song and sang it in the ceremony. I ended it by saying, "I's married now!" and everyone laughed. Melanie, Daddy Clyde and my mother came but my other siblings didn't show. It was on a Friday and one of my brothers who could have come because he had no job wanted to apply for emergency food stamps since the Northridge earthquake happened days before the wedding. The statement was even caught on tape with Melanie telling my mother that Jake and his girlfriend felt that the food stamps were more important. Those niggas didn't even live in L.A. County.

Nate and I dropped Candace at a friend's house and we went on a two day honeymoon to Hollywood. We also went to Universal Studios and stayed in a hotel on Sunset Blvd. That was the beginning of a long thirteen years. First I locked my keys in the car because Nate let it slip that he glad that was over because he thought that he would lose me if he didn't marry me quick. I immediately got a knot in my stomach. Why would he think he would lose me? I didn't understand. I was in love and I know it was a quick three months but I was thirty two and I had no time to waste. I told him that I thought we got married so we didn't have to live in sin.

The wedding night was a bust. His pipe wouldn't work and I thought I've been cursed for fornicating. I prayed for forgiveness and figured I'd tried the next day, but there was nothing. I tried not to let it bother me, but I was preoccupied with the hot sex that we had for the two months we were sleeping together. I asked Nate if there was something wrong and he said he was fine. Fine! I wasn't but I said nothing. However, I did buy a book on intimacy and sexual techniques that we could learn together as a new married couple. I showed him the book and he shut down. He didn't want any part of it and I couldn't figure for the life of me why. I read what I could, trying to break down the wall that had developed in about a week's time. He became distant and began to avoid going to bed at the same time. He often would sneak in the bed when he knew I was asleep. I pretended to not notice and sex was when he wanted it and as long as he got his it was fine. I didn't say anything for a while because I feared him becoming more distant and I didn't like the feeling of being abandon yet again. He was okay as long as he got want he wanted and I always delivered in good fashion. I was the good wife, with the fabulous food and the perfect home life and child who was respectful. I dressed him well and learned to shave him so he didn't have to wait for the barber chair. I was a virtuous woman that he could be proud of but I was lonely as ever. I told no one of the problem to avoid the backlash of I told you so and you married too soon. I missed my friend and I wanted him to come back. I enjoyed a lot of the things that he enjoyed like going to concerts and listening to old school music. I also loved to hear him play. I would sit while he practiced. He would sing my song and I would feel butterflies in my stomach. I loved him so much, but the connection was somehow broken. I got by, by thinking of the good sex we had before married and would pray silently asking for forgiveness for fornicating. I felt that this was my punishment and I dealt with it alone.

I was thirty two and I asked Nate when he thought it was a good time to start a family. He didn't have any children and I promised him at least two because I was so old. I wanted to stop trying at thirty five. He was okay with trying a.s.a.p. and I wasn't mad at him. I prayed to God for forgiveness for my past sins that I had not shared with my husband and to bless me to conceive a child for the man that I was crazy about.

It was *boom boom* time and I felt that he would give it all he had. I was wrong, it felt like he was just doing his business but I said nothing. I convinced myself that I could deal with it and I was longsuffering. I had developed patience and I knew what he could really do.

Six weeks after the wedding, while at work, I started to smell fruit cocktails. I walked around the cubicles looking to see who was eating them and could not find them anywhere. I also started liking milk which I felt was strange since it always made me sick to my stomach. I told Cher that I thought I was pregnant and she didn't believe me. I knew my body and I had had enough pregnancy to know what it felt like. On the way home from work, I stopped and purchased a home pregnancy test. After dinner, I took Nate in the bedroom and told him what I suspected. He didn't believe it either so I pulled out the test. I went in the bathroom and peed on the stick. I stay in there while he knocked on the door and asked if it was pink. I told him to wait, that the time was not over, but in fact it was positive and I was in there having a Holy Ghost fit. I was praising Jesus name and thanking God for grace and mercy. After about what seemed like forever I came out of the bathroom and gave Nate the stick. He was so excited that he slipped and fell on the bed. We both were laughing when Candace came into the room and we announced the news. She wanted proof and we were glad to show her the stick. Candace started to dance and sing that she was going to finally have a brother or sister. Nate jumped up and got on the phone to tell his family in New Orleans that he was going to be a dad. I looked at them both and I couldn't be happier. We were a family and it was about to grow by at least one for now.

My first visit to the doctor was routine and everything was fine. I began to have issue with a few things though, like my husband scent, Hated it. His voice hated it and his touch hated it. I even avoided looking at him because I couldn't stand the way he looked. I had sex with him because it was a wifely duty, but I took no pleasure at all. Often times I would make sex sounds to excite him so he would come quick to get off me. I apologized often because I knew it was wrong but I couldn't stop myself. We were only married for three months and I would start an argument to have a reason for him not to be close to me. That worked for a while then it was to let Mister do his business. I had no idea that I was destroying his morale and that I would pay for it later.

I was now six months pregnant and I started having complications.

The doctor called and I rushed to his office. Apparently, my antibodies were fighting the baby like a virus. I was crying and I thought I would lose it. I went through many tests and was later taken off work early. My feet were swollen and I was tired all the time. I had to go to the doctor every week to be monitored and it was like pins and needles. I prayed constantly for the Lord to protect our daughter and that she would be okay. I already had a name. Jennifer was going to be okay and I knew it because God said so. I was forgiven and I was now at peace. I would dream of an old lady tending to her flowers and I stopped to talk to her and she told me that she was tired and then died while leaning on my shoulder. I didn't understand the dream, but it didn't scare me. I was at peace and I welcomed the visits in my dreams. The roses were beautiful and they were so real I could smell them.

I decided to have a Cesarean after seeing the many videos on vaginal births. I made up my mind when I heard of the complication and the threat to me and Jennifer. I knew I was a woman and I didn't needed to go through all that pain and trauma to prove it.

Sandra gave me a baby shower and I didn't get many gifts and didn't care. I had purchased so many things that Jennifer didn't need anything.

While shopping at Wal-Mart in highland I noticed a truck in the parking lot full of snow. I was talking to Nate and then I just stopped. He took one look at my face and took off running. I carefully took my time and made a perfect snowball and after he got about one hundred feet or eight cars away, I throw the ball and when he turned to look it hit him right on his ear. He was shocked that my aim was so good then he felt the coldness of the snow and quickly knocked it from his ear. I laughed so hard I started to wet my pants then I crossed my legs to avoid a mess. I looked across the parking lot and notice that we had an audience and laughed even harder.

I went to visit my sister Melanie and she told me that she was having a baby too. I thought to myself, not again. She was going to foster Daddy Clyde's sister daughter who was a drug addict and was not able keep the baby after it was born. It was nice that the baby would come to family, but I thought not everyone is mother material and from the struggles Melanie had with her own three I thought it to be a mistake but I smiled and congratulated them both. We were saying our goodbyes when Daddy Clyde hugged me and when he let me go, his hand went across my nipples that were really sensitive and I lost it. I started to yell at him and told him if he ever touched me like that again I would kick his ass. I was so upset that I scared Nate. He didn't know what to think. I got in the car feeling violated and shaken up. I told him never to touch me again. Candace and Nate rode in silence and I was quiet too. I started telling them what happen as a child and I had never told anyone that he tried to molest me at the age of ten. I told them that he was a pedophile and I didn't trust him, not even with his daughter. Candace asked if that is why she never spent the night over there and I said that and the one time she did sleep over, Daddy Clyde would come into his daughter's room and watch them sleep. Candace said she was so scared she stayed up the whole night.

That nigga's nasty.

There were a lot of issues and concerns that I had with my family, but I was called the trouble maker until they needed help. Charles even tore away from the family because he knew it was dysfunctional and didn't want to have any part of it. He spoke to mom, but that was it. I missed him but I was not going to force him to see me. I knew how to give him his space.

I found that Charles was a big influence in my life and my guardian angel after the death of our father. He became my father and my support system. He taught me how to cook and to defend myself. For my sixteenth birthday, he took me to the Manns Chinese Theater to see Stars Wars and after that, out to dinner at Loves Restaurant. Whenever we went for walks, he would walk on the outside of the sidewalk and when I asked him why he told so the man could protect the one he loves against harm. I felt loved and safe with Charles and respected his opinions totally. We would listen to music and his favorite was Earth, Wind, and Fire and Chaka Khan. I also knew when to give his space. It was nonverbal but I knew and I would excuse myself whenever I got the cue.

Charles had to drop out of school to raise us, but he read a lot. He finally decided to go the Job Corp to earn his GED. When he left I was heartbroken but I didn't show it. I couldn't be selfish and I was his sister, not his daughter. He deserved his freedom and I was not going to get in his way.

Charles returns to find a different person in me. I was in love and he was not happy with my choice. I didn't understand why not at the time, but to say it was because he was too dark was not a good reason. Charles might have felt betrayed and our relationship became strained. We would argue and he would threaten me many times but when I felt he was being unreasonable, I refused to back down. It always ended peacefully with agreeing to disagree. One time we were arguing and he called me Tuna which was his pet name for me and I told him not to call me that and he never did. I wished that I had never told him that because I missed him calling me Tuna. I realized that it was a term of endearment and it was forever lost. We drifted away and he the join the Navy but changed his mind after boot camp. I never found out how he got an honorable discharge, but that was Charles. He was my hero, my mentor, guardian angel, and my father. He met and married a wonderful woman, who was able to calm him down. He was happy and I was happy for him. Sue and I quickly became sisters and I felt God had given me the sister that I had longed for. She taught me how to be a lady and to calm my own temper down. Sue was another one of my guardian angels. I would come and spend the night with them and they always made me feel welcomed. She worked at a department store and was Charles anchor. He had all his necessities met and all the comforts that he deserved. I was truly thankful for her. Charles was a very passionate man. He stood six foot tall and Sue was five two. They were the perfect couple in my eyes. Charles was cruel to Sue but she was a strong woman in a small package and she knew how to tame the beast in Charles. They would complement each other and I saw the true dynamics of their relationship and it worked well for them and they didn't care about what others would say. Charles worked at a warehouse and made a lot of money back in the eighties. He was in shipping and receiving and he had control of the entire place. He knew where everything was without looking at a manifest. I was impressed with his mind and I mimicked myself to his way of thinking. He was my hero.

Charles was my role model of what a man was. I think that's why I started dated and eventually moved in with Anthony. He and Charles were good friends that met at the warehouse. Anthony idolized Charles and I thought I could finally have a man, a companion and husband that would treat me like Charles treated Sue.

After about eight years of married, Sue was diagnosed with breast cancer. Charles was laid off from his job of as many years and with Sue sick she was on disability. They kept it from me for a while but finally told me when it became terminal. I was devastated and I prayed for a miracle. I would watch him give her shots and take care of her. I loved my brother and wanted to be with him. One day I went to his house and I was suffering from Bronchitis. He was in the kitchen when I got there and before Sue could stop me I interrupted him in the middle of hitting the pipe. I had done it before and I was in so much pain that I asked for a hit. He asked me what I knew about that and I told him enough. He gave it to me and I showed him just how much. After the first drag,

I was on cloud nine and the pain was gone. I didn't know that that would be the biggest mistake I would be making. He was in pain and I was in pain. We became the blind leading the blind. After months of being partners in crime, frick and frack, it was apparent the our relationship had went from siblings to crack addicts. We argued about the size of the rock on the pipe and I valued the relationship so I told him that I thought it best if I didn't get high with him anymore. He respected my decision and we parted peacefully and he was my brother again.

He did get another job but it didn't last long and he met some unsavory people at the railroad. This one guy was a biker dude and I had come to his house to surprise him with a birthday cake and he was in the room doing drugs. I went in to say happy birthday and he went off. I told him that he should be ashamed of his self and that this was not him. I was told to get the fuck out and to mind my own business and I replied this was my business. He was my hero and I was not going to turn my back on him when I saw he was in trouble. The guy left and he did calm down but I was scared. I was still hitting the pipe but it was in secret. My freak would come out at night and his freak was open whenever the feeling hit him. I sat in the room for a while with him while Sue kept Candace. They both consoled one another while they probably thought we were in the room killing each other. I don't know how long it took while I watched Charles finish getting high. It was torture to watch his lips around that pipe while wishing it was mine. I was licking my lips but I had made a promise not to get high with him because I valued the relationship and I loved my brother. I pretended to enjoy myself the rest of the night but what I wanted to do was go and get high. Candace and I stayed the night but the next morning I was up and out to get back to San Bernardino to cop for myself. Even though I was able to finally get to sleep, the cravings were overwhelming and I compensated with alcohol until I passed out. I left Charles and Sue and raced home while the craving intensified. I tried to keep it from

Candace, but she knew I was not myself and thought my mood was from the argument with Charles the night before. When we got home, I made some excuse about having to go to the store because I forgot to get something and I left Candace home along. My freak was out in the daytime and I couldn't control it. I felt guilty but I would give myself selfish excuses that didn't even make sense. After putting Candace to bed, I would leave the house sometimes three and four times in a night. I was out of control. God took care of her in my dementia.

Sue was admitted into the hospital for pneumonia and I went to see her. Charles told me that they were releasing her and I knew what that meant. They didn't even give her pain medication or oxygen. It was around Thanksgiving and I gave Charles money to go to the store and purchased food for a dinner and he was cheap with the meal and pocketed the money. He was taking a long time to serve the food and we got into an argument about when Sue should eat. I didn't understand that he was afraid and that he was thinking the same thing I was thinking, that they sent Sue home to die. Sue was getting upset and I thought it best that I left. I went to their bedroom and sat on the bed beside Sue and just leaned on her shoulder. I apologized for the arguing and she stated that she understood. I told her that I loved her and that I was glad the she was in my life. I told her she was the sister that I always needed and that I would come back when things calmed down. I sat silently while my head rested gently on her shoulder and she said she knew and that enough was said. I kissed her and left. As I walked into my apartment the telephone was ringing. I answered it and it was Charles telling me that Sue was gone. In shock, I asked gone where and he repeated in a trembling voice she's gone. I asked him where he was and after he told me I told him that I was on my way. Candace and I ran back to the car and went back to Los Angeles. I almost flipped my car going too fast interchanging to the 60 freeway from the 215. I got control of the car or Jesus took the wheel and we made it back there in record time. Charles was sitting alone and Sue's family was looking all crazy. I knew that they lost a sister, but she was in good hands while Charles was left alone. I hugged him and tried to console him and he just repeated that she was gone. I told him that I wanted to see her and he directed me to where she was. Candace wanted to go with me to say goodbye and I allowed it. Sue was her only real aunt and I thought it was a good idea. I told her that she was still Aunt Sue and to think of her as sleep. We went into the room and I regretted taking Candace in. I thought she was going to look sleep, but in fact she still had breathing equipment taped to her mouth and her wig off. I didn't know she was wearing a wig. I kept my composure and made it alright for Candace who was eleven at the time. I said goodbye and kissed her on her forehead and Candace did the same. I thanked God for giving me the time I got with her. She was a true sister. I later took Charles home where he just lost it and I could do nothing but sit there quietly while he grieved. He practical tore up the room and I cried for him because I knew that he was in great pain and there was nothing I could do. Sue died on November 27, 1992.

Chapter 21

The next day in the mail was the long awaited Social Security check and I advised Charles to turn it in because she died thinking that they would give him another one with his name on it. They didn't, and then Sue's sister took half the life insurance money that Charles had paid for because they put her as beneficiary on the policy. Charles was swimming in debt and they with their money hungry asses robbed him of the money to get back on his feet. He lost the love of his life and then got robbed by her sister. That's a big monkey to have on your back. I arranged the funeral and took him to the store to purchased gloves for her hands. He even mentioned me as a special friend in the obituary which was an honor.

To this day, Charles stays in touch with mom but doesn't call or see anyone else and I miss him so much. I respect his space, but I would like to have a relationship with him and for Jennifer and Nate Alex to know my hero, their Uncle Charles. I tell stories of my life with Charles and they wished that they could see him. I tell my mother every time I talk to her that I miss him but out of respect she will not give me his number. I will continue to respect his space but I miss him so much. I pray for him daily and it's not a day that go by that I don't say a quote that I learned from Charles my hero and biggest, but not the oldest, but best brother. My mentor forever.

Jeff would come around to show off the new toy he purchased and enjoy the praise he would get for doing so well. I was happy for him and would tell him I thought that he was doing well, but I knew that his now wife, Pamela, was the catalyst for all that he had. He was smart to listen to a woman who had a plan and knew how to work it. I admired her business sense and learned by watching. Education was the key and I had that. I think Pamela didn't like me because I refused to put her on a pedestal.

Deidre was in her own little world still living in Illinois even though her husband had past several years ago. She was left with five kids and her in-laws that needed her to put them on a pedestal of their own. She would visit and she would often state that she didn't remember her childhood. Rodney was the oldest and he was a man without a job. He was an entrepreneur. He had several businesses but never had a paycheck. I never knew how he made it but I refused to show him my license and I told Nate that if asked direct him to me. Kevin was the youngest and he is handsome and he used it. He's been married and divorced twice with children left behind for the mother to raise by themselves. I tried to tell him that he needs to be in his children's life and to stop blaming everything on his ex-wives. Jerry was the mean one, and selfish as hell.

It was all about him. He was the rasta weed smoking, much respect to the queens, then offer to drink their bath water, type of guy. Lord, help him get his head out of the smog cloud in L.A. The last is Jake. I think he was the one wounded as I was as a child. All he wanted was to be loved. He had some problems but out of them all, he was the one with the most progress. God truly blessed him with grace and mercy. I think he and I had the shield of protection and angel guarding us from our wild spent and misdirected youth. Jerry was later arrested and charged with lewd acts with a minor. The thought of drinking bathwater finally got the nigga in trouble. I never knew what he did and I didn't ask, but I know he now has to register every year like Junior. Weak men. What a waste.

Jennifer was born on November 28 1994 and she was cute and totally healthy. I gave the middle name from Cher my closest friend at the time and I liked the way it sounded, Jennifer Denise Richard. She weighed 6lbs and 14 ounces. She had milk chocolate skin and a head full of hair. God out did himself and I wasn't mad at him in fact I was truly grateful. The nurses would fight over who would take care of her. She was a good baby with the jaws of steel. She nearly ripped my nipple off when I tried to nurse her. The nurse gave me a pump and the breast milk came out pink from all the injuries Jennifer had inflicted. I decided that not all women could breastfeed and figure that was not one of the gifts God give me. After four days in the hospital, Cher came to get us to take us home. Nate was at work and couldn't drive my car because it was a five speed. I was settling at home when he arrived and we just look at the blessing lying in the crib. My hormones had begun to get back to normal levels and I was in love again. I didn't even mine taking Nate to work that night even against doctors order but I was careful not to rip a staple.

Nate at the time was working two jobs, probably the hardest he worked in his life. He went from a part time employee for the school district to a full time temp for the Post Office. The money was good and we had everything we needed.

After six weeks, I was ready to return to work. I had arranged for Cher's mom to watch

Jennifer and I pay her fifty dollars a week. I felt that was a good rate because she wasn't doing anything anyway and it would put extra money in her pocket. Cher and I's relationship was not as close and after a month her mother demanded more money. I told her for the rate she was asking I could take Jennifer to a qualified daycare center where they didn't smoke around the children. I packed Jennifer's things and walked out the door. How dare she count my money and say to me that we could pay more with all that money that we made. Greedy heifer. She just lost two hundred dollars of extra income. I guess Cher will have to pitch in as usual. I bet she wished she would have kept her mouth shut.

I took Jennifer back home and told Nate what had happened and that I needed him to call off from the part time job to watch her. He called and quit the job. I went to work and was talking to a coworker and he told me that he had two daughters and his wife was a stay at home mom. He was a Christian and every time she came to the job the girls were always nice and neat. I gave him my number and told him to call me later that night to give me a chance to talk to Nate about it. When the coworker called, Nate and I had talked, and his wife had agreed to the fifty dollars a week. Cher was not happy but this had nothing to do with her. I decided not to be swindled by her money grubbing mother but it had nothing to do with her character. Or did it? She started to ignore me and say she was too busy to take breaks. At first, I didn't think anything of it until June. My birthday month and the office always had a potluck and a cake for which I paid two dollars a pay period to be a part of. Cher and another coworker were in charge of the festivities and the month was almost over. I went to ask about the potluck and Cher looked at me like she had no idea of what I was talking about. I walked away and hear her and the other coworker laughing.

I was crushed. This was my buddy stabbing me in the back. I spent a lot of time with her and her boys. I loaned her money when she was in needed. I protected her when she was in the mean streets of L.A. and she does this. I was not embarrassed I was devastated. It hurt so bad I cried at the job and when she came to gloat, I told her that I would have never let anybody do that to her and she claimed that she had nothing to do with it and that the other coworker was to blame. I told her that she could have least warned me of the animosity so that I would not have been blindsided. She realized that she was her mother's child and the relationship was over. We were in a clique so we still had lunch together with the group and she became another coworker in my mind. She would talk about her antibiotics and her urinary tract infestations and I would tell her that she shouldn't talk about those things because people were talking about the rough sex she must be having with the exotic dancer. She was proud of the pictures of his penis that she took and showed them to the girls at the office. She became a well-dressed loser and I quit talking to her. At least I was happy in my relationship and I didn't feel like I had to make up story to talk about my sex life. I was a lady.

Months had past and Nate's position at the Post Office was over and he was out of work, unemployed. It didn't matter because he was going to get another job. I was encouraging, but I had no idea that he had no clue of how that affected him. We decided after a month that he should watch Jennifer to save some money and he could work on his music. I would come home to laundry and Jennifer would still be in her bed clothes from the night before. There was no dinner cooking and he was a cook in the military. I spoke to Nate about my concerns and "I'ma" moved in with us. *I'ma do this, I'ma do that*, but it never happened. We went to marriage counseling at our church and the Pastor told him that the roles were reversed for the time being and that he had an obligation to contribute. Nate was very agreeable but nothing changed. I would come home to the same bullshit and I gave him every opportunity to fix it. We began to argue all the time and I told him that he better be glad his baby was cute or I would give him a bus ticket and tell him to take his ugly baby with him. That stopped the argument as we both started laughing, but I was serious. I prayed for guidance and was told by God to take him home. I knew I heard wrong. I had to be hearing wrong. Leave my job of security. I had changed positions and became a floater and went to different offices to work which gave me a lot of experience. I ignored the call and was disobedient. The problem had gotten worse. We moved from the Condo and rented a house where Nate could be in the house playing his music and caring for Jennifer and it still got worse. When I couldn't take it no longer I was willing to listen to God and his command and I told Nate that we had to move to New Orleans. Nate was adamant about not going back to his hometown and I asked why. It was the music, always the music when I told him it'd be good no matter where you are. He told me he was not going. I told him that we either go together or he go alone. I was not going to be taking care of a man. I didn't want to make him comfortable. This was the man that was mad when I bought a twenty five cent pack of gum on our first date. Now I was paying all the bills. Something was definitely wrong with this picture. What was I teaching Candace? That it was alright for a man to have no responsibility while I took care of everything?

I don't think so.

He called home and I heard screaming in the phone. His mother thought it was a good idea. It was settled. I made the plans and it was in motion. I scheduled the pod to be dropped off, I called my brothers to help us load it and I gave my job two weeks' notice. We bought plane tickets for the girls and gave 30 days' notice to the owner of the house. I was excited and I felt no fear because I felt that I heard the Lord not once but twice to take him home and it made sense. Nate was a fish out of water. California was too fast for him and he needed a confidence boast and I thought he could get it in New Orleans.

Chapter 22

February 28, 1996, moving day.

We had packed the pod and locked it then went to a hotel. That next morning, we put Candace and Jennifer on the plane and headed out on the road. I drove all the way because Nate didn't know how to drive a stick shift. I knew that was a lie. He didn't know how to drive at all, but I didn't say anything. I figured once we got settled, I would bring it up and deal with it. We arrived in New Orleans on March 2 and my finger had swelled from the trip. My wedding ring was strangling my finger and it was turning purple from trying to remove it. I told Nate that I needed to find a jeweler to get it cut off. It seemed that his attitude was different. He was not attentive and this was serious. I got the phone book and call Bell Promenade Mall. It was a Sunday and the Mall was about to close. I asked Nate if he knew where it was and he was moving slow. I grew impatient and scared that we would not get there in time, so I took off and left him. His mom figured I didn't know where I was going but I could follow directions well. She didn't know me. I was a survivor. I was on my own for a while and it appeared that I was on my own now. I did make it to the jeweler and was relieved that the ring was cut off. I returned to his mother's house and his brothers and their wives were there. I was pissed as hell but said nothing to Nate about the abandonment that I felt. I got something to eat and excuse myself because I did drive by myself from California to New Orleans alone with the nigga who couldn't drive. I would deal with him in the morning. We stayed with his mother for six weeks too long. Nate had got a job and then caught Pneumonia and I took the off work order to a job his job that he had for about a week. I told his boss that he was a good employee and I hope that they could wait for him to get better. They did and I was grateful. Within the six weeks I met several family members who sized me up and compared everything to California. I wondered what the fixation was with California. We were average people just with a different accent. We joined his mother's church and I was interested in the word and Nate was interested in the music. I started to see that the music was what kept him coming and not the word. After church they would have roasted Preacher, Choir members and Deacons. I realized I was in a house of backbiting Christians. My sister-in-law Maggie was the ring leaders. One evening she talked about my mother-in-law so bad, I felt embarrassed. She often called her husband Mister Phillips and I didn't get the joke. Who was Mr. Phillips and why was Nate's brother, Sam, allowing her to call him that? Later I found out that Mr. Phillips was rumored to have fathered Sam and I didn't find it funny. That was my mother she was talking about and hers too. Her indiscretions were hers and she should have been talking to her children, but it was nothing to be joked about. I figured that this nature of weak men ran in his family and if it did I might have made a mistake. I began to think I was wrong when I told my mother that Nate was all man and that he might be stupid. As my daddy used to say I done got rid of the rats now here come the roaches. Where were the nice family that I met at Christmas? They had gone and I was left with manipulators, secretive and vengeful greedy people who put on a facade of good character. Candace was told by her new aunt that she was too young to be called aunt and to call her Rachel then Nate's sister Netty's son walked in the house and said hi to his aunt and she replied with, "Hi baby." He was older than Candace. I saw Candace's face and I begin to fume. My baby was hurt and there was nothing I could do about it, but take her aside and tell her not to let it hurt her but I knew it did. That incident destroyed what could have been a good relationship. Her husband, James, Nate's younger brother loved Jennifer and at that time they didn't have children and she stated that she didn't want children. James would pick Jennifer up and give her kisses on her neck. Jennifer's body would go limp to receive all the love that her uncle had for her. She was a year and some months with beautiful eyes, thick gorgeous hair and chocolate skin. Rachel, James wife would often look at Jennifer with daggers. She hated all the attention that Jennifer was receiving from her husband. It bothered me and made me feel uncomfortable because I felt that Jennifer would get the wrong message. I had no reservation about James because he was a good man; I just knew that all men weren't good. I told Nate that it bothered me but I never told him why and his usual response was that it was fine. I never told him about the looks that Rachel gave Jennifer but he wasn't blind. He just chose not to address it and neither did I.

My mother-in-law loved the casino and we would on occasion go with her. On this one trip I ordered a sprite with olives and I enjoyed it then I ordered another then finally I asked for a cocktail of olives. My mother-in-law was laughing at my attack on the olives but I thought nothing of it at the time. The next day we went grocery shopping and I looked up with a mouth full of Olives. I realized what I was doing and recognized the symptoms. I was pregnant. I couldn't wait for Nate to come home from work to tell him what I suspected. I told his sister, Netty, that I thought I was pregnant and she said that I wasn't pregnant and that she was going to the store to get me a pregnancy test. I told her it was her dime. I waited for her to return to go to the bathroom and I was ready to explode. I took the test and came out with a quickness the test was positive. I didn't even have to wait long. It changed while I was still urinating. That's how pregnant I was. I must have gotten pregnant when my foot touched New Orleans soil. Everyone was happy for another baby in the family and I had fulfilled my promise to Nate for two children.

I went to the doctor and found out I was six weeks pregnant and it was the exact weeks we had been in New Orleans. The baby was conceived in my mom's bed with her blessing I thought. She would always ask where he was conceived and I would tell her she already knew since she had walked into her room at six in the morning as Nate was coming in a downward stroke tearing it up. We had the window open and just a sheet over us. Nate melted into me with shame as he buried his face in my breasts. I could feel him tremble as he came and I could do nothing but laugh silently. Mom was embarrassed too, but that is what married people do. She left the room and Nate jumped up and got the comforter off the floor and covered up. His mother returned and made mention of the comforter being back on the bed. I responded by telling her I got a chill. Nate was mortified and I was pissed. How uncouth, even I knew not to enter a room without knocking. If she was embarrassed, it served her right. She should have been happy that it appeared that her son had a healthy sexual relationship with his wife.

Nate was happy about the news that we were expecting another baby but we needed a place of our own. I convinced him that we needed to start looking since we had a steady income and could afford to live on our own. I was ready to leave the nest, now desperate to have a place of my own. I was tired of the non-verbal innuendos, the attitudes and the silent treatment. They didn't know I didn't respond to hints. You had to be direct with me and say what was on your mind not throw a basket of laundry at my feet and walk away. I did fold the clothes but I then got up and went to Home Depot and purchased a large plastic trash can then had a family meeting with Candace and Nate and told them that all our dirty clothes are to go in the can. Nate missed the message because he continued to put his clothes with the house and his mother, mad at me, didn't notice that it was only his clothes. I didn't take notice that not many of his clothes were in the loads that I cleaned.

One evening, he came to me all booted up asking where his underwear were. I told him that I did the laundry and there was nothing in the can and he looked like he had shit for brains. I dismissed him by continuing to do what I was doing spending time with my girls. Fuck him. He could go to his mama for his underwear. He ain't nothing but a mama's boy and it was becoming more and more evident.

I did love him and I felt different with this pregnancy. I was clingy to the point that I felt weak and vulnerable. His smell, I loved it. His voice, I loved it. I loved just watching him and wanted to be with him all the time. I wanted to be put to bed with sex and wake up to it. By the end of the pregnancy I was head over heels in love and delighted to tell him that he got his son.

We discussed names and I didn't want to name the baby after Nate. I wanted my son to have his own identity. I finally compromised and changed the middle name.

Nate was okay with that and he had no choice. I was thinking about the child and he was thinking about how it made him look. Nate Alex was born on November 22, 1996 to two long waiting sisters ready to love and protect him. Candace was now seventeen and Jennifer would turn two in six days. This year her birthday fell on Thanksgiving. It was symbolic for me of the confirmation that God was pleased with me. I knew I was not perfect but I wanted to live right.

Candace was there to help me with the children and I was always cautious not to put the children on her. I never asked her to do for the children, but she helped anyway that she could. She often joked about having siblings and asked what took me so long. I would tell her it was not up to me. I had to be blessed with a husband and then the children would come if it was God's plan and it was.

I had given Nate a son and although he wasn't named exactly as his father, that was his son. When Nate Alex was eight days old, Nate went to help a friend out with some music. I wasn't feeling well, but I told him to go. He promised that he would be back by 7:00 pm. I wished him luck and he left. I was getting worse and by 6:00 pm, Candace was begging me to go to the hospital. My head was hurting bad, but I tried to wait for Nate. 7:00 came and went and after 8:00 Candace was pleading. I gave instructions for Candace to lock the door and put the safety on. "Do not open the door for daddy and tell him to go to the hospital". I knew Nate, and he would not come right away if he went in the house. I went to Rite Aid and took my Blood Pressure and it was high by both numbers. I then drove to the hospital and after talking with the triage nurse was put in a bed. I thought that this must be serious to get a bed this quick. I was hooked to monitors and the tests began. I asked the nurse to check the lobby to see if Nate was waiting because I knew that his shyness was going to take over and he would just seat there like he was waiting for permission to move. She came back and told me that no one answered to his name. I heard the doctors talking about my condition and they kept asking the same questions. She is how old? She had a baby when? And blood pressure and heart rate is what? I began to worry so I asked the nurse if it was serious and if I could die.

Her silence spoke volumes and I started to get scared. I thought about my children and especially Candace. She was in a city where she had no family and I didn't want Jennifer and Nate Alex to be raised by such mean people. I asked for a phone and called home. Candace stated that daddy had come home two hours after I left and that he should be at the hospital. She also told me that he was mad that she couldn't let him in. I assured her that I will explain everything. I told her to call Maggie and asked if she could come and stay with her to help with the children. I hung up and called my mother-in-law's house and Netty answered the phone. By her tone I knew that Nate must have been there and that she was mad. I asked if he was there and she said yes and nothing else. I asked if I could speak to him and she said hold on in an even nastier tone.

Nate got on the phone and I asked why he wasn't at the hospital? He didn't answer my question but asked me why I locked him out of the house? I couldn't believe that he was not concerned about me and that his feelings were hurt and that he felt disrespected. I told him what was going on and he repeated the question and I told him that I knew that he would sit at home scratching his fucking head if he went into the house. Uh oh, I thought, that didn't come out right but I was scared and he was worrying how it looked. Fuck his family and what they thought. I needed my husband and what hurt the most is that he needed them. I told him to forget it and hung up. I called Candace and she said that Maggie was there and that everything was alright and not to worry about them. I made a call to California to my mother. I told her that I was not well and I might die. I asked her if she would get the children because they deserved better. My mother paused and said nothing and I asked if she was still there. My mother began to talk about how I had moved all the way down there and that she was through raising kids. I started to laugh and told her I will speak to her later. I had to get off the phone before I disrespected my mother, but the thoughts of my laughter said it all. What kids did she raise anyway? She has nine kids that ran like a pack of wild animals, fending for themselves and latching on to anyone who would give them some food and attention. I realized that I was screwed or should I said my children where screwed. Candace didn't have anyone on her father's side of the family that would care for her the way she deserved. What would become of Jennifer and Nate Alex? They were too young to take care of themselves and how would they be treated by a family who thought their mother was a California Bitch. I started to pray for more time. I promised that I would care for my children and to raise them right in God's eye for more time. I started thinking of scriptures about the desires of my heart. That Jesus died for me and by his stripes I was healed. I cried out for Jesus to save me and make me whole again. I told him that he gave me a son because I was worthy to raise him and that I needed more time. I told him that I was not finish and that he was not finish with me.

And it was finished.

Around 7:00 am, the nurse came and unhooked me from the monitors and told me I was ready to be released. She said that they didn't know what happened but all my vitals were back to normal and that I would be fine. I knew that the Lord answered my prayers and I was truly grateful. I don't remember the drive home but as I entered the door Candace came running to me and I told her that God saved my life. I told her that everything was going to be alright. She told me that daddy never came back home and that Sam called and ordered Maggie to leave them alone. I repeated to Candace that everything was going to be alright. I checked the children and told her she did an awesome job of caring for the children while I was away. I thanked her and held her tight. I loved her so much and knew that God gave me a chance to prove that love, and to show my children how much I enjoyed being their mother. I went to my bedroom and began packing Nate's possessions, his clothes and other personal items. I didn't however mess with his keyboards that were erected on a stand instead our closet where he used to escape. I didn't want him to think that I intentionally broke something. I wanted a clean break and I accepted his decision to stay with his mother. I figured he made his choice and I wasn't going to beg or seem desperate. It hurt like hell that my marriage was over and that I was in an unfriendly city where no one knew my name. I knew that this was not what God brought me to New Orleans for but I was not going to dwell on what was happening. I was getting state disability from California for maternity leave and I knew it was not going to last forever but I didn't worry. God had just saved my life and I was confident that he was going to bring me through this.

Chapter 23

As I sat on the bed, Nate walked into the bedroom and all I could do was look at the foot locker sitting in the corner. His face looked sad and lost and I wondered why. He had control of the events that lead to this but somehow he managed to put the blame on me. I was the one who was in the hospital all night alone and scared. He started to speak stating that he didn't know what happened and he never did. Many times that came out of his mouth "I don't know" like it excused him from any responsibility. "Candace should have let me in," he said and all I heard was Lord it was that woman that you gave me. My Nate was being Adam and I was not going to hear that. I told him to get his things and go. He in his arrogance and pumped up confidence from his mother's house fueled with attitude and I didn't care. I was a survivor and I knew I was going to be alright. He took his things and Candace came to me and sat silently and I felt her thoughts. What were we going to do? He was the one with job and the money. I reassured her that we would be fine and comforted her in my motherly embrace.

It was a couple of days before Nate called claiming to want to see his children and it burned me that he put emphasis on his children excluding my daughter Candace.

The hatred was building in his mind and I was not going to be broken. I did wonder how he could be easily swayed to turn on me in less than a year of moving to New Orleans. I thought we were put together by God and that we worked well together, but it was obvious that I got the message wrong or this would not be happening. Oh well, I thought it is what it is.

He came into the apartment and it was a different story. He pleaded with me to take him back and that he was sorry. I sat there with a stone heart. I was not going to give in to this emotional blackmail. He told me that he wanted his family back and that it was not supposed to be this way. He told me that I was his world then I turned and asked him what planet had he been visiting because he hasn't been home in months. What hold did his family have on him? Why was he afraid to take up for me or to be supportive and to choose us? I told him that she had never called another man daddy and that meant something and for him to kick my child to the curb because he was not her biological father. He's coming to see his children. Bullshit, this was not about me; it was all about my daughter's self-esteem and feeling accepted by another dysfunctional family. She was constantly being picked over by family members and I had had enough. It was time for me to express how I felt and it wasn't pretty. We were a family and we were happy. Yes, we had problems but what family didn't? We stuck together and he got here and he jumped ship. I told him that I thought he was different and I wouldn't have never let my family sway me away from what we had. I told him that he was the only daddy that Candace had relationship with and he threw it away as if it meant nothing. I told him that he was heartless and I didn't know him. I started to cry because the words burnt through me like acid. I wanted the best for my daughter as well as my other children and here I brought them to the unfriendly Chocolate city, the big Easy. What a joke! I brought my children to hell and it was my responsibility to get them out. God had governed me over them to protect them and to teach them and I was not doing my job correctly, but that was changing. My strength grew and I would be victorious and then God spoke to me not to harden my heart and just like that, I looked at him differently and we both cried. Nate dropped to his knees and I fell with him in prayer for God to give me the strength to forgive him. I didn't want a hardened heart. I wanted the love back; my home without chaos and all this confusion. I did love him, but I felt abandoned by him and the trust was damaged. He told me that he was wrong and that he wanted to come home. I looked into to his eyes and told him that I will guard my child and that I will not let anyone fuck with them, my money and I will not be called a bitch. I had gotten tough and he was going to take it or leave it. He accepted it and we cried some more.

Peace was restored to my home and I would attend his mother's church where everyone knew your name and your business. The sermons were adequate when the head Pastor spoke, but went all over the place when any of the Assistants would preach. It was like I could see their demons. I remember one minister talked about the issue of blood in his sermon. I was in pain. I couldn't take it anymore when he said she was cauterized. All I thought of was a hot poker shoved up into my special place. I jumped from the pew with Nate Alex in my arms and Candace and Jennifer in tow. I walked to my mother in law's house which was a block from the church. I went into the bathroom and thought that nasty nigga done talked about the issue of blood so much that my cycle came down. That minister had a lust demon and it showed in his sermons, the way he look at the women and the things he said, not to mention the smirk that he constantly had on his face. I wouldn't be caught dead in a room alone with him, I knew that much. Another minister had an angry demon. His wife would flinch whenever he was around. She would check his face to know when to speak and when to shut up and makeup never covered as well as she thought it did. I knew a wife beater when I saw one and I'm not talking the undershirt that was supposed to be worn under dress shirts. The last minister was funny. He spoke so fast that I couldn't make out anything he was saying except the name of a character in a children's book that loved honey. He would talk about his past life when he would be in the world as if he missed it or he was glad his wife didn't give up on him. I felt that he was heartfelt and that he had been through a lot and was grateful of God's goodness.

The abuse of Nate's family continued, but with him by my side it didn't matter. They would say off handed things about California and I would ignore it. References were made to the ways I did things differently down to the way I ate my food, but I would say nothing. I would talk to my husband about it and he would say that they didn't mean anything by it. I bit my tongue so much that I felt like I had a stomach full of blood. One of Nate's uncles used to hit on me. What kind of hoochie did he think I was? Netty even took me out with her and provided me with a date and I was in shock. That was my husband's sister. I figured that loyalty was dead in this family. I turned him on them left him hot and bothered and went home to my husband and channeled all my sexual frustration into a wild night of sex and pleasure with Nate. I told him everything the next morning and that I didn't know that Netty's boyfriend's brother was going with us. Netty even had him drive me to the club in his car. I told my husband that I flirted with the man out of guilt and I had to get it off my chest so the devil couldn't use it against me later. I couldn't read Nate's reaction and so I was through with the matter. I chose not to ever go out with Netty again because that was not my kind of party.

I felt she was trying to put me in a trick bag and I was too smart for that. I felt that his family was wolves and I knew I had to keep them away from my sheep.

Nate and I moved to a bigger apartment and I started working for a temp agency while I met more colorful characters. I was convinced that New Orleans was a place of idiots; slow people who were okay with the status quo. Black people on one side and whites on the other. I would hear things like black people don't do this and that, but I was black and I was doing it. I took my child to the park to fly kites, we went bowling, and I liked steak.

I met a girl at the temp job and we became friends, my first friend. For a year in a half, I knew no one but Nate's family and I was not getting a good impression of the people of New Orleans. Tasha and I would bring different food to work to share. She would bring southern food and I brought everything else. Mexican, Italian, even egg rolls. We would share experiences and the other women would talk about us. I didn't care but Tasha did. The men would call me Miss Marilyn and the other ladies by their name. One day we ordered food from a diner and my plate had Miss Marilyn on it and one of the girls said what made her special to get Miss in front of my name and a guy stuck up for me saying it was the way I carried myself. I felt good that he noticed but I blessed that food real good before I ate it just in case.

Tasha was living with an older man and she was very young with several children. She needed him to supplement her income and he did whatever he wanted. I would offer her my testimony of how God brought me through a lot of things including drug addiction. Tasha was in disbelief. While we spoke, another girl overheard me. I started to share with her too. She was gripped on my every word while I spoke of my deliverance from crack cocaine. She told me how she was struggling with the drug and I told her when she got tired of the life she was leading God would be ready.

I worked there for about four months when the drug user told me that she will no longer be working there after the week was over. I looked at her and told her that my work here was done. When I got home from work, I had a message on voicemail from the State of Louisiana offering me a job with Human Services. I thought of what I had told the girl and I started praising God for the blessing. I was at the temp job and I had done what I was sent there to do and now it was on to better pastures and I was ready. I gave two weeks' notice and the supervisor was disappointed because he had chosen me to get a permanent position. I thanked him, but declined and the manager said I didn't have to give the notice if I want to leave at the end of the week. I did accept that to find adequate daycare. My mother-in-law had been watching Jennifer and Nate Alex and I wasn't pleased with their care but I couldn't afford to put them in a qualified daycare center. They would come home with fire ant bites that were never explained and Nate would tell me not to say anything. I would pray extra hard every time I had to take them over there but we needed that money. Now I could afford to put them in a daycare center and demand an explanation if my child had a mark on them and

Jennifer was almost three and talking. I knew she would tell me if she was mistreated. I visited a lot of Daycare centers and found one that I liked. I was ready to go back to work.

My mother in law was not happy and I told her that I wanted the children to get socialization and that wasn't a lie. I did. I wanted them to be active and to play with others. They loved Olivares and the staff loved them. They would tell me that Jennifer and Nate Alex were good children and I was proud of them. I knew that I was doing my job right.

The relationship with Nate was okay, if no conversation, sex every once in a while, I got more looks from guys on the street that I got from my husband and being left alone every night to go play music in his music room. I prayed all the time for change but nothing happened.

Chapter 24

Candace was in high school now and she was in her senior year at a Magnet school. She was smart and got in with a great essay 10 out of 10 correct. I was proud of her and my mother-in-law would praise her to her friends. She had a hard time liking me but she knew I was a good mother. Even though we moved I kept Candace in that school until she told them that she moved and she was transferred to the school in her district. That was after her senior pictures were taken and her class ring was purchased for the magnet school. I went to the school and pleaded with them to let her stay and they refused. I told them that one of their star football players lived where we did. I walked out and said it is what it is.

Candace had lost her virginity six months ago to a guy she met at the local market. He started off nice and then my mother intuition kicked into gear. He had escorted her to a home coming dance and she looked beautiful. We took a lot of pictures and she reminded me of Julia Roberts in Pretty Woman the night Richard Gere took her the Opera. They went on a couple of more date and I noticed that Candace was getting serious. I asked her had she met any of his family and she stated no. I looked at her and said "Don't you find it strange that he hasn't showed you off to his family. You're a California girl, pretty and smart." He must have had something to hide. I told her to take her time and guard her Hope Diamond. A few dates do not make a relationship. I told her that the only thing you get from fornication was an unplanned pregnancy and a STD. She accused me of trying to ruin her life and I told her I was trying to shield her from pain that was avoidable. She didn't want to talk anymore and I knew that she was thinking of this guy she knew nothing about and she gave him her special gift for what, a few dates?

While at the store, the guy Candace was dating came and picked her up and Nate let her go. I returned to find her gone and I yelled at him. Why did you let her go? I asked and he looked at me like I was crazy. I hadn't talked to him about our recent conversations. He didn't know but I wasn't hearing it. He was supposed to protect her and here he had his head in his keyboard's ass if it had one and let Candace go to make the biggest mistake of her life. I was livid and I knew I was unreasonable but that made no different. I went in the room and cried.

The next morning, I was afraid to come out of the room but I got the courage. I said good morning to Candace who was sitting on the sofa. She said nothing but I went to prepare breakfast. I was in the kitchen when Candace came in there to make a call. She sounded agitated on the phone and I knew something had gone wrong but I said nothing. Ten minutes later she came to make another call and she told someone on the other end to tell the guy to return her call then slammed the phone on the receiver and stormed out of the kitchen. While I tried to figure out what to say, she was back on the phone. I told her to hang the phone up and she didn't listen. She dialed the number and my heart ached. She started to bang the phone on the receiver and I grabbed it from her and she fell into my arms and cried. All I could say was I know. I held her and let her cry. I gave her all the time she needed and I stood there waiting for her to recover. I would have stayed there for as long as she needed me to. She broke away and said I was right and if I was satisfied. I was in shock, how was it my fault? I did everything I could to tell her it was not right. She was seventeen and I taught her everything she needed to know. She was yelling and having an Adam moment and I was not going to take it. I told her that she better get a grip. She had a choice and now that she made it and thought she was grown she better deal with it and don't call him again. My voice meant business and she knew it. He never called her again and I thought my daughter who I taught so well give away her Hope Diamond for a chicken dinner and a movie. I felt bad for her but she was not going to put that on me, not after I stayed up half the night praying that she made the right decision. It went to show me that we all have freewill and choices to make some good and some bad. I just hoped she used protection.

Now Candace was attending a high school in Jefferson Parish on the west bank and she had a lot of friends. She seemed happy and I allowed her some space. She was growing up and I taught her all that I could teach her and it was time to let her spread her wings and grow. I found out later that she was spreading more than her wings. She started getting wild after graduation. She was grown by all accounts and I was watching her self-destruct. Nate's distanced no longer was on my mind. I had other things on my mind, my first born. Candace was coming home at all hours of the night and I would tell her that there was nothing out there but trouble at that time of night. She heard me, but continued to stay out late. I told her that she was wearing my patience and that she had to be considerate of the rest of us. She heard me, but did not listen. She started college at the University of New Orleans and I thought she would do well. I warned her to stay away from credit cards and wild parties while she looked for just that. I continued to pray for her and hope that she would be alright while she found her way. She was grown and I refused to spank or punish a grown woman so I tried to convince her to think of us. She kind of calmed down and started to come in earlier and I was relieved.

Candace had offered to watch Jennifer and Nate Alex while Nate and I went on a date. She stated that we needed some quality time and she was right. Nate Alex wasn't his happy jolly self and Candace assured me that she could handle him. I was worried but I didn't want her to think I didn't trust her with the children so I went. We had fun at Bally's casino, but not to gamble, we saw Confunkshun an Old school band that we both loved. Love Train, Fun, Let Me Put Love On Your Mind. We were grooving and having a ball. After the concert we came home to Nate Alex high with a fever. Candace was in a panic and I was trying to calm her down and care for the baby. I striped his clothes off while running a lukewarm bath. I knew I had to get the fever down and I had no time to lose. The baby stopped crying and gave the smile that melted my heart.

After about twenty minutes of playing and his fever down, I took him out of the water and wrapped him in a towel. While I sat on the bed to dress him, his body went straight as a board. I couldn't get his attention and he didn't make a sound. I yelled for Nate to call 911. Nate got the phone and stood clueless as to the number. I told him to stay with me and repeated 9 1 1. He then dialed the number and then couldn't speak. I grabbed the phone and immediately told what I had done and what was happening now. I was told that the EMT was in route and to say on the line. I cradled the baby until they got to the apartment. The Paramedics took over and I stayed out the way and went into prayer. Something was wrong with my baby and I wanted God to fix it and I commanded to devil to take his hands off my child. I said it with authority and they ran out the door with Nate Alex. I told them I was riding with them and didn't take no for an answer. They allowed me to ride in the cab even though I wanted to see my baby. Nate followed in the car but was too close and the EMT had to stop to tell him to back off. He did what he wanted. I told the driver that he was hard headed and just get to the hospital. I had no time to the think of the world according to Nate. My son's life was in jeopardy and he was not going to get my attention right now. I kept my cool and listened to every doctor that spoke. I wanted to know what was happening but I stayed out of their way. I was a praying woman that night or should I say morning. I remember that God gave me a son because I was worthy and I rested on that. I amazed myself as to how calm I was and how well I could hear. My senses were sensitive but I couldn't tell you what Nate was doing. I don't recall even seeing him until the baby started to make his usual cooing sound and then I saw him watch me comfort his son. I never mentioned how he lost his mind in a crisis. It didn't matter my son would be fine.

He had a febrile seizer due to the high spike in fever. The doctor explained that there was no damage and I would have to watch him and any fever until he turned two then no worries. We were able to take Nate Alex home and found Candace and Jennifer asleep in our bed. I told Nate not to wake them and we went to their room because I wanted to stay with the baby.

I enjoyed my job and I liked my boss. I found out later that we shared the same birthday and she liked me from the start of the interview. She knew I was from California and would often have staff meetings away from the office so I could see the city on the East bank. Monthly, we went to a different restaurant for lunch, Stuart Andersons near Canal Street, Pappy's in Gentilly, The Hilton by the Riverwalk and Jack Dempsey on Poland in the ninth ward. My husband was shocked that I knew the city so well. I would surprise him with a dinner date to experience his own home town. We always did Bally's and enjoyed concerts featuring Cameo, Denise Williams, Midnight Star, Cece Peniston, and many more. We went to Boomtown, which was my mother in law's favorite casino, to eat lobster when it came to town.

I started to see that New Orleans was a great city; I was just put in a fish bowl with Nate's people but once I started working at my filed of choice which was social services I met some wonderful people. The money was decent I always said little becomes much in the Master's hand and it was.

We were able to purchase a home after three years of moving to New Orleans. People would make comments about how well we were doing and I would say that the lord was blessing us. I led and

Nate followed until his family got into his ear. He stopped coming home for our traditional Sunday family breakfast. Nate Alex would give me percentages and fractions of the family that was at the breakfast table. It broke my heart that we weren't whole but I was proud of my son for being so smart. He was only in kindergarten. When I told Nate what he said, he heard but he didn't listen. He continued to please his mother and neglect his family. We would get into arguments about his distant attitude and I told him that the children will get older and they will see that he is not there. He heard me but he didn't listen. He was Eve and his family was the Serpent whispering into his ear.

Meanwhile, Candace was attending UNO and racking up debt in secret. She was also having unprotected sex and got pregnant. I was hurt, in shock and highly pissed. She was grown but she still lived at home. What was she thinking? She was taught. She knew what made babies. How could she do this to me? If I wanted another child, I wouldn't have got my tubes tied. Nate Alex would only be three when the baby was born and Jennifer five. I told no one, I was ashamed and scared for my daughter and she acted like it was no big deal.

I remember telling her not to get pregnant before she got married because I saw many birth certificated with asterisks where the daddy name was supposed to be. She didn't listen and my worst fears came true. One day at church, someone congratulated me before she had even started showing. I was trying to get my mind right and I found out this heifer was telling the good news with no shame. I never even met the father. I had nothing to say because I knew nothing.

I was embarrassed and I feared a tough road for my child but she had to go through it and I knew it and I didn't want to feel her pain. I didn't want to see her in pain. I didn't want to give her a baby shower but was pressured by my in-laws who were cheap anyway. I think I spent more on the food than she got in gifts. I tried to be there for her, but the pain was too great and I now knew what my mother felt when I got pregnant. I called her and apologized after twenty years and I was sincere. I now knew what my mother felt. God also showed me what I was doing to Candace and when she went into labor, I went into labor too. I was in so much pain and my good friend Veronica who accepted the title of Godmother was laughing at me. She said she knew that I loved that child and that's a lot of love. I stood in the hall with my back pressed against the wall in agony. Candace tried to get ghetto in the delivery room using profanity and I told her to knock it off or I was leaving. It was bad enough that she was having a baby by herself as if she could raise a child alone. That shit was hard work.

After a lot of pushing she had to have a Cesarean section because the little angel tried to come through the birth canal with his hand on his head and got struck. I said he was thinking and that broke the tension in the room. I was scared for my daughter and I was not handling it well. I was mean and resentful until God revealed that he allowed this to save her life and that I had to let her care for the child alone as my mother did me. That was some tough shit and she lived with me. I couldn't throw her in the street, so I was going to be a part of that struggle and I was not ready. Ready or not here it comes.

Veronica and I looked at the baby through the window and we both turn our heads sideways in silence. I then said I could do something with that and we both broke out laughing. My grandson's head was cone shaped from being struck in the birth canal longer than normal. Veronica said, "I don't know" and I assured her that I could while praying that I could.

Nate went into surgery with Candace because I couldn't fit the scrubs and came out like a proud father saying that his daughter was fine. I was relieved, but I couldn't get my mind out that head. While in the hospital, the low life poor excuse for a little penis called the hospital after his cousin and sister came to visit and take pictures of the baby but he never showed up. I never met the man who fathered my daughter's first born and that was a shame. Children should be protected, provided for and loved or at least acknowledge and that bastard didn't even bother to come and see his child. What did I expect? She even told me she was just kicking it and I asked her who was she? What did she do with my child? I loved my grandson but I made her take care of him. I didn't feed him, I didn't change him. I didn't watch him but I did have quality time with him where I sat and rubbed that cone head to get it to look normal. He was a pretty baby once the head was shaped. I often would have to yell to Candace that her baby was crying and to come and see about him. Nate Alex would mock me and that infuriated Candace. I made her applied for Welfare and she came back humiliated and in tears and all I could ask if kicking it worth it. I thought it was better than I told you so.

I made a compromise with Candace to go back to school and not have a job and I would take care of Sweetie Peetie. She agreed. She registered at the community college to studied communications. She was bringing me A's and I thought she had a chance until she got greedy, wanted more money and went and got hired as a bank teller. Her grades started to slip and she started giving me excuses about not having her grades yet. I told her that I was not going to be watching her baby if she was not willing to show me the grade. Later she told me she got fired from the bank because she was a "no show, no call". Well, she went in some two hours later and had nerves to be mad that they fired her. I had to ask her if she was that gullible. She was talking about wrongful termination. I wanted to knock her out, especially after she told me her dilemma the night before and I told her to go to work. I got her a car to drive around in, I was watching her baby, and she lived in my house. What the hell did she want from me? She had a bad attitude and frankly, I was tired of it. She was messy and ungrateful. She was no longer a minor. I didn't have to take this shit. Let me make my own mistakes as long as you feed it, clean it and take care of his basic needs. Bull shit, I wasn't going to be in the belly of the whale like Jonah. God said let her take care of him and I did one better. I asked her what she would have done if she had to pay real bills not the pennies I made her pay, because my brother Charles always told me it cost to live in this world, and she said smugly that she would have went to work. I said okay.

The next day, I called all the shelters for

teen mothers and she barely made it as a teen. I found what I thought was a good one and proceeded to interview the director of Liberty House across the river. I came home and told her to pack her shit. She looked at me like I was crazy and I told her she wouldn't be living her anymore.

She got some things for her and the baby and I took her to her new home. I made sure that she had a place to lay her head and I was gone. I was in so much pain that I cried all the way home. I hated leaving Sweetie Peetie, who was going to tell her that her baby was crying? How would I know that he was alright?

I had to pray to be strong for the hurt I felt and the backlash from my in-laws. *People in California were heartless. How could I do this to my child? Like she never made a mistake.* Nobody understood God's plan. I was being obedient. Candace needed to be on her own then maybe she would appreciate how good she had it or not.

I know one thing; I didn't have a baby that I did not care for. When she was a baby and I was on welfare I sacrificed for her and all I heard was what about me. How bad I mistreated her and I thought I was nothing but good to her. I gave her time, I educated her, I provided for her and loved her and most of all I didn't abandon her. She enjoyed the sympathy and Nate gave it to her. He didn't understand how I could do it and with the serpent in his ear that made it worse.

Nate got Candace a job where he worked, so that she could save money to get her own place and she ended in the sack with a married coworker. I was mortified and embarrassed for my husband. That girl had so many monkeys that it was a shame.

She had a low self-esteem when all I did was praise her when she was right and chastised her when she was deceitfully wrong.

My house was crowded and my family was falling apart but I was still standing on God's word. It was painful and lonely, but I was not going to stop being in God's will. I was still standing.

One day we were going to the New Jazzland amusement park in New Orleans East and we decided to see if Candace and my grandson Sweetie Peetie wanted to go. We got there only to see Candace sitting on the stoop smoking a cigarette in a house dress, nappy house shoes with a rag wrapped around her head. I was pissed. Instead of her having regretted her decision, she fitted right in to the hood life. If anyone had told me that this was to be, I would not have believed them. I sat there fuming and wondering where was my grandson? Candace finally noticed that we were there and she took her time to get to the car out of sheer embarrassment. She knew she was busted, looking like a derelict.

I started to think that maybe I was wrong and I began to weaken. She came to the car and I quickly came to my senses after she had the nerve to defend why she looked so bad. I told her that we had to go and that we just came by to see how she was doing. I didn't even bother to invite her to the park. The children enjoyed the park and all I could think about was my baby and how it came to this. Nate seemed to not have a care in the world. Why should he? He way stuck under my wing and provided for. I began to think that this might have been normal for him judging from his family. It didn't matter, it was my family too, but it didn't have to be my children. That curse was going to be broken.

Days later, I went to see Candace and we played a friendly game of Gin Rummy. I was checking out the surroundings while I heard one of the tenants talking to her child like he was a sailor. She was using language that was not fit for any child to hear. I was taking score and I started to write out a contract of the rules for her to come home. She agreed and after talking to Veronica she thought it best to stay with her in Metarie. It was fine with me as long as she was not in that place. Veronica was a good friend and Godmother and she stepped in when ever needed.

Candace was still working at Nate's job and had ended the affair after I went to the man at the employee picnic and told him he had a lovely family. I told him that if he as much as looked at my daughter again that I would have no problem talking to his wife about his time away from her. All the time I had a smile on my face, but he got the message.

As I walked away, I greeted his wife and told her to enjoy the rest of the day. I returned to my family and also enjoyed the rest of my day. I never told Nate what I had said to the coworker and I guessed he never said anything either. I felt that Nate should have handled it but he didn't like confrontation even if this was in his back yard.

Chapter 25

I felt that his coworkers would start to disrespect him and I found out that they did when on a dinner cruise aboard the Creole Queen, another coworker sat with us and began in light conversation stated that he knew that Nate was having fun with my breasts because they were huge.

He talked about me like I wasn't there and the lustful tone was disgusting. I began to shrink as I waited for my husband to defend me. I started adjusting my clothes and peeking to see how much cleavage was showing. Nate said nothing, but had a stupid grin on his face and in my discomfort I changed the conversation to the good food.

I managed to keep a smile on my face but I felt verbally molested and dirty. I was hurt and unprotected. My submission to Nate had put me in a bad place and I began to lose respect for him. I loved him so much but I felt the love was not mutual. As we sat there, the coworker went a second round. This time I was not going to keep silent and when the word nipple came out of his mouth I went off. I quietly told him that since my husband was too dumb and stupid to protect my honor I had no choice but to protect myself. I told him to take his ass to another table and get my breast and my bedroom out of his fucking mind. He tried to apologize, but I was not hearing it. He didn't mean to offend me. I didn't know what kind of women he was use to talking to or about but I was not the one.

I took Nate out on the deck and told him that if he didn't learn to speak up he might as well bend over and take it up his ass. I felt that he was being punked and it had me open to be punked too. Nate said he was sorry and I told him he was and went back inside. It was quiet on the way home, you could have heard a pin dropped and I wished an anvil would have fell on that nigga's head. I figured it was time to forget being submissive and to take care of myself. No more keeping my mouth shut because he didn't want to make any waves. It was long overdue for a fucking hurricane.

The children loved Mardi Gras and I often went without my husband because he said the he was through with that, but let a concert come up and he was out the door. He never valued time with his children like they were only my responsibility. I had them because he didn't have children. I didn't want to raise them alone, but he was not hearing me. Their need was my responsibility. He would tell them to "Go to your mama," whenever they needed help. When there was a decision to be made it was always *go to your mama.* Jennifer came to me while I was cooking and asked if I could fix her closet shelf. I told her to go to her father who was doing nothing as usual and she replied "Why? He will only tell me to come to you" This was becoming a problem, so I went to Nate and asked him to fix the shelf and he did. So I thought, until I heard a commotion in Jennifer's room. I went running in there to find her buried under supplies for her pet hamster. I was furious. I made sure she was alright and then fixed the shelf and she looked at me and said, "Now you see why I come to you." I held her tight and thanked God that she was not hurt. I realized that I was not the only one losing respect for my husband but the children also knew that he was not dependable.

At Christmas time, my children would get dollar store toys from their relatives while the other children received more expensive ones. It reminded me of my Uncle John and how he gave my siblings and me frogmen that blew bubbles in the tub and the cousins got remote control cars and beautiful dolls.

Fuck this shit. It was not going to happen to my children. My children were smart, but my son and grandson got guns for Christmas one year and others got leap pads and computer discs. My niece saw my face and told me that Netty, her mother, knew I didn't allow my children to play with guns. So, she knew. That was a big statement. I was an outsider, an outlaw and my children were being sacrificed to hurt me. My mother-in-law came to me and said she couldn't find a rice cooker anywhere and that's why I didn't get a gift. I felt like tellng her that it was alright I would just keep the expensive perfume that I got her and we would been even, but I didn't, I smile and told her that it was okay. I was okay. I was used to not getting presents so why should this be any different. I knew how they felt and I knew it would have been phony anyway. Thank God she knew how to cook and Christmas wouldn't be a total waste. Later I spoke to Netty and I told her that if her heart wasn't in the gift giving mood not to bother to buy my children anything. The next year, my children didn't receive a single gift from anyone and that was the last time we had Christmas away from home. My children didn't need to feel rejected, like outcasts and unloved. They had everything they needed. We purchased an above ground pool, they had a trampoline and a swing set in the back yard. My children were happy and I refused to let vengeful people put monkeys on their backs. I heard laughter in my house, not fights and I intended to keep it that way.

I continued to go to his mother's church where I was mistreated by all people the Pastor's mother. One day, my family and I were eating at the church hall for communion and she came over to our table and hit me so hard on my arm saying hello. I winced and said hello and then she went over to where my mother-in-law was sitting and they had a good laugh. I was at a church function and I thought am I not safe anywhere. I had to pray hard about what had happened and I learned to watch my back. Candace would see the things and asked why I continued to go to that church and I would tell her that we will stay until daddy leaves or God tells me different. That made her angrier and she felt that I was a fool. Our relationship was strained, my husband and I was not speaking if he wasn't getting anything out of it and my only comfort was my children's laughter and my faith in God that he would see me through this and that he would not give me more than I could bare.

Oh a week later the Pastor's mother died of a massive heart attack.

God don't like ugly.

Even though my mother-in-law was mean to me, I still felt sorry that she lost a dear friend. I participated in the re-pass, a meeting after the funeral to celebrate the life of a loved one who had die, by making my famous peach cobbler. I prayed that the Pastor's mother repented for the incident that happened a week earlier. Candace didn't understand why I was working so hard to give my all, but I felt it was what God wanted me to do.

Chapter 26

I went back to business as usual. I worked hard and ministered to my customers as I determined eligibility for welfare and condition them to become gainfully employed. I wore two hats in my position as an Eligibility/Find Work worker for the State of Louisiana. I enjoyed my job and got a lot of satisfaction from my job. I heard a lot of things from my customers, some who were not shamed to tell me how they got the rent paid. I often secretly prayed for them because I knew what it was like to be a recipient. I thanked God for not having to do some of the things that I heard. I would go the extra mile for my customers and was treated unfairly by the higher ups at the job.

The stress was getting to me and I became sick. It started with minor pains in my body until one day I couldn't walk. One morning my hips locked up on me and I was in excruciating pain that I couldn't even go to work. I went to the doctor and was prescribed medication the added seventy five pounds to my alright two hundred fifty pound five foot five inch frame which made it even more impossible to walk.

I went to several doctors and no one knew what the problem was. I was prescribed Zoloft, but stopped taking it after my husband notice that my sex drive was gone, plus it didn't get rid of the pain and I wasn't depressed. I was a child of God and I couldn't be depressed. I would drag myself to work every day, do my job then go home and take care of my family before collapsing into a pain coma with muscle relaxants and pain medication. My life had ended as I knew it. I would stare at my shoes in the closet because I was no longer able to wear the four inch heels that I use to wear. None of my suits fit and I had to buy bigger clothes.

I had heard about a medical procedure that would help me lose the weight that I lived with all my life. I went to a couple of group meeting about the Gastric bypass. I started researching the procedure and felt that it was an answer to my problem. I felt that if I wasn't so heavy that maybe I could walk again. I went back to my doctor who got offended that I was considering the procedure. I told Nate about the procedure and he was not on board with the idea. I ended up throwing all the material away because I couldn't go through with it if we were not in agreement with it. I dealt with the pain and medication and endured the pain in prayer until one day Nate met me at the door saying he was alright with it. He had seen a documentary about a singer who had the procedure and she came out of it alright. I thanked God for given him something that he could relate to. A musician of all people. I got back on the computer and began printing information about the procedure. I went back to the groups to learn everything about the procedure so that I was well informed when I presented it to my doctor. I was with an HMO and needed her to refer me to a specialist and she kept stalling while I got worse. I wondered what I had done to get this condition that I didn't even have a name for. I pleaded until my doctor gave in and she didn't even submit the paper correctly.

I was denied the procedure and I filed an appeal and was denied again. The denial stated that I had no medical reason for the procedure, not even the hundred and fifty pounds over my normal weight. I was considered morbidly obese and it was not considered medically necessary. I began falling to sleep at my desk at work and would often wake to Z's all over my computer screen that I spent have the day trying to clear it up to make my computer work. My work was failing and that was more ammunition for my supervisor to reprimand me for.

My customers would often write letters to my supervisor about my good customer service and how I had helped them. I would get awards for my performance and then get shot down for a mistake I made on a case. I would keep my cool as I was being berated and question about anything from giving a customer a second chance to the clothing that I wore and the amount of sick leave and vacation I had on the books. I told my supervisor that I had a life and I took vacation because of it. I told her that I had an illness that was undiagnosed and that when I didn't feel good I didn't come to work. I also told her that I chose to look professional as I was advising people to look for work and I wanted to give a good image to my department. I answered all her questions and she took it as I was being insubordinate. I couldn't win for losing. I begin to get written up for all kinds of things none which were true. I needed Gods help and I needed it now.

My stress level went through the roof and I thought I was losing my mind. Nate didn't understand and refused to see what was happening to me and I had no one to talk to but Veronica who no longer worked for the agency. Her schedule was hectic and she had her own life and problems. I kept a lot of things to myself until I couldn't take it no longer. After about a month, I couldn't take it anymore. I made an appointment with my doctor who also handed my appeal incorrectly and I got into an argument with her and she told me to leave. Days letter I received a letter from her office that I had been fired as her patient. I was lost. She was the doctor that knew about all that I was going through. God lead me to another doctor that had me tested for sleep apnea and my test results were horrible. I had stopped breathing sixty six times in the sleep study. I went for another appeal and after a conference call with my new doctor was given the approval to have the Gastric bypass. I had fought so hard because God had told me that he had it but I had to be obedient and do as he instructed. I didn't know why I had to do the things I was doing but I did them. A coworker at the job would ridicule me about my fight but I had heard from God and I didn't care what she thought. I pressed on and I won. She said that she would be shocked if they approved my surgery but I was faithful. I knew what God had told me. He had this and I believed him. I didn't worry anymore I just did what I was lead to do. I took the letter to her and when she read it she threw it on the desk and I just looked at her. She looked at me puzzled and I stated that I was waiting for her to look shocked then picked up the paper and walked away praising God.

My surgery was the buzz of the office when I requested time off, and I lost a lot of so called friends. I became the office gossip even in supervisor staff meeting told to me by a very good source. I was looked at funny after a rumor surfaced that I ate myself that fat to be eligible for the procedure. It didn't bother me because I had Jesus on my side but that was some mean stuff.

It was the day of the surgery and Nate had to go to work. I told him to go and that I was not alone. I had Jesus with me. I was joking with the anesthesiologist and he commented on my good spirits. I told him that God had this and I was out.

I woke up in the recovery room to everything going well but I was not surprised. Jesus was with me. I began losing weight at record speed and I did everything as directed except for a few things that I found that kept me from getting nauseous like eating a few hot tamale candies to settle my stomach.

I knew I was not supposed to be a size six and I didn't starve myself trying. My body came to a healthy size fourteen and I was satisfied. I did get a little better but I was not able to exercise like I wanted to because my body would swell up from the still unknown condition. I was able to walk upright and without pain but weight lifting was out of the question. I ended up losing a lot of the forty four G's that I had for breast and I didn't mind however I went from big full teardrops to flat donkey ears. I would lie on the bed and my breast would go under my arms that were also waving in the wind. My body was hideous without clothes on but I looked nice with them on. I would apologize to Nate for the wrecked body and he would respond that I was fine. Everything was fine with Nate, so I didn't know how he felt really, but I was healthy and that's all that mattered.

Our relationship continued to drift apart even though I looked and felt fabulous. His family was still mean to me and I just stayed out of their faces. I didn't need to be the one to make them do things then they would have to repent for later.

Nate spent a lot of time over his mother's house leaving me alone. I would get compliments and flirty gestures from other men whom I would then start talking about Jesus and my husband with. I thought that would tone it down but it only made me a conquest. I diverted every situation that I could only to be told what I had on yesterday and how good I looked today by other men then to have my husband ask me if an article of clothing was mine or Candace's. I would get so frustrated that my husband didn't see me. I had never looked so good and he didn't even see my transformation, but other did.

One night while sleeping, the devil entered my dreams and a security guard at my job was giving me compliments. I played with his advances and began to moan in my sleep. The moans were so loud that I woke myself up. I began to pray that God took the temptation from me because it appeared that I was getting weak. The next day at work there was a woman security guard and she spoke of being blessed that God had answered her prayers and that was now her permanent position. I went to the elevator praising God and telling him good looking out.

A bullet dodged.

I spoke to Nate about the dream because I was concerned and I wanted my husband and he said everything will be fine. I've heard that before. That was high on the charts with *I'ma* and *I don't know*. I remained prayed up and joined the church choir. I knew that God was working things out and I had to just be patience which I made a mistake and prayed for.

I would release stress by baking and

praying over the lives of people I had met that day. I soon started taking my baked goods to work and made a lot of money selling the product I had made the night before. God gave me a gift and I thought of the scripture that my gifts would make room for me. Some of my coworkers were rude and the supervisors would pick on my so bad that I thought that if I started my own business I could make a fortune. I had perfected the praline and my brownies were the bomb. I would make sixty dollars a day with a basket of my treat on my desk. I figured I could do much more if I spent all my time at it.

I spoke to Nate and he was in agreement however I didn't know that he was passive aggressive at the time. I then spoke to my Pastor and told him that I feel that God had given me a sign to open my own business. I told him that I plan on renting a space in one of the church member's restaurant and he said nothing of the character of said member. I went in with both feet quitting my job and purchasing equipment that I had delivered to the restaurant and lost my shirt.

The member robbed me blind and I had no one to blame but myself. The Brownie Lady was out of business as quick as she started. I quickly regrouped and took the lost. I turned the other cheek and began selling on the street. People crowded my brownie mobile, a 2001 Hyundai Santa Fe that I had paid the payment with the product that I sold. My pockets were fat with all the money that I had made and I was stress free. I looked like a drug pusher with all the money I made. Nate was impressed and I felt I had found my calling. The people at the State building in Harvey Louisiana were calling me on my cell phone to bring them my treats.

My former coworkers, the haters, quickly put a stop to it when someone called the revenue and taxation agency on me. As I left the office one day they jammed me up outside and gave me a warning that if they saw me selling at the State building or anywhere else, I would be arrested. I didn't want to break any laws and I didn't want to go to jail so I had no other choice but to stop. With the money shortage, I and I alone started to feel the pinch.

Nate was oblivious to the money situation, not because I hid anything but because he didn't listen. I told him that I had made a mistake and he would say everything would be fine. I was sinking fast and I put a bandage on it by asking Candace to move back in to help with the bills. I felt it was a win, win situation because she was also struggling after forcing my hand to kick her out.

I later found an opportunity to open my business again and Candace help me complete a Business plan for a loan, but my credit was no longer a A-1. I had a couple of slow pays and could not get a loan. I went to my Pastor for a $1000 startup loan and he told me he had to talk to the deacons and I knew that was protocol. The building I wanted was across the street from the State building and on a major thoroughfare. I had all my numbers right and was ready to go and I had not heard anything from my Pastor. The owner of the building couldn't hold the building any longer and I needed an answer. I went to my Pastor who told me that the deacons slammed the idea and said to ask later. Later? There was no later, but what could I do? I continued to sell at the church because the members loved my goodies and it was some money.

One day a deacon was talking about how I had mastered the Praline and said I should open a shop and I told her I tried but that the squashed my idea. The deacon looked at me funny and I asked him when he thought they would make a decision on my business plan and he didn't know what I was talking about. I told him what the Pastor said and found that he didn't know anything about my proposal. I quickly changed the subject and stopped talking as I sold to another member. What did I just do? Then, I thought, my spiritual father lied to me. I was heartbroken and hurt. How could he betray me? In my mind I kept hearing he is a man. He is a man. Men lie but not my Pastor.

I asked for a meeting and asked the Pastor why he lied. He didn't have to lie. "No" would have sufficed. He was more interested in who told me but I refused to divulge the information which made him more upset. I left his office feeling lost.

Chapter 27

I took up smoking again. How could I be smoking again? I was delivered from these filthy things but I had to calm my flesh. I haven't had a cigarette in three years since the woman's conference. I was devastated and I felt alone. I knew that God would understand because I was hurt and abandon yet again. Nate didn't make me feel any better. He not only made me feel guilty, but claimed that that was why he didn't kiss me, which was a lie he didn't kiss me because he didn't know how to. We had never gotten to perfect our kissing since we were married and I just assumed it was because of the curse of fornicating before married and I had no right to complain. Soon after a couple of sermons about buying my product and slimming on the offering by the members I stopped selling all together. We were sinking fast and the help that Candace provided a bit of aid, but we were too far in debt and had to file for bankruptcy. I would go over what I did wrong to put my family in such a mess. I felt guilty and Nate let me. He had me where he wanted me: submissive and alone. I started going back over to his mother's house where he showed that I was now in line. I felt victimized by my own husband. I was alone, while they mistreated me and I just took it.

Every Sunday, the Pastor had something else to talk about. One week it was long hair to short hair. The next week it was hair color. Yes I wore weaves and I wore my hair short. I lightened my hair because I had a lighter complexion and dark hair made me look washed out. I began to get angry and think he should pay more attention to his own fucking wife and stop looking at my changes and then I would have to repent.

By this time, my mother-in-law had gone home to be with the lord. And I know she repented and God her forgiven her and accepted her into his Kingdom. I knew that for a fact because I was the one who cared for her in her last days. We became good friends and I took her to every appointment after she was diagnosed with terminal lung cancer. I researched her condition and she was confident that I knew all the questions to ask. She told me she wanted to fight and I was willing to help her. I had written down all the information for Nate's siblings but they were to angry and hateful to look at it or maybe they were too scared to face the facts that their mother, the matriarch of the family, was dying. For her birthday, they gave her a birthday party at the church hall that resembled a wake. It was about two hundred people there and it was clear that my family and I were outsiders until they needed her oxygen tank changed and I was the only one who knew how to change it and it wasn't because they were not shown. I walked across the stage in a suit that my mother-in-law loaned me, my hair moving with grace and my posture straight with dignity and change that tank with a quickness.

I didn't care anymore, she was my mother and I took care of her like a daughter would. She in turned acknowledge me by calling me her nurse and that she was truly grateful for all I do. I took a bow and went back to my table looking like a single parent because my husband sat at the family table that didn't include me or my children. When she died, the mess got worse. I was excluded from the business of her estate but the other wives weren't.

My husband signed over his interest to the two pieces of property without my knowledge and I was dissed at the funeral by Maggie when she stepped in front of me in the procession as we enter the church and Nate had no other choice but to let my hand go. I stood there with my head down not because I was beat but I was fighting my flesh not to kick Maggie's ass in the church. I had had enough. She was the hater of them all. I think her husband admired my strength even though I angered him so she was jealous. I stood there until she let all the family in then walked in herself and then I proceeded. Nate did look for me and told his niece to move and then motion me to come and sit with him. I felt his love and felt that this would be a new beginning. That day,. he sang the best I've ever heard him sing and I was proud.

After Mom's death I cut off all connection with the Richard Clan and live a quiet life with my family. I was now the matriarch of the family and I was determined to set a good example. I continued to go to the church because my husband was one of the musicians and I had to represent, but my spirit was not there. I was so exhausted hearing from the pulpit slams at my character and the children were still too young to notice and Candace had already started going to another church. I guess after the Pastor saw that his little tyrants were not affecting me anymore he denounce speaking in tongues saying, "speaking in tongues ain't nothing."

He started criticizing the apostolic faith. He knew I was born and raised Apostolic. He went there and I was appalled. He cut me deep. I had a decision to make and I made it. I asked for another meeting and discussed the sermon with him. I explained that I had heard the assistant ministers talk about speaking about tongues with disbelief but never him. I told him that if he felt that way then I could no longer attend the church. He replied saying out of all the sermons he preached that I was going to let this one overruled all the others? I told him that speaking in tongue was a gift from God and it was the one that edified the spirit. I concluded the meeting with a simple goodbye. Later, the fast talking minister came over to visit and we started to talk about tongues and he stated that tongues were from the past and he related it to the city of Babel. I thought these people were misguided. The day of Pentecost was so that all tongue understood one another and the city of Babel was so communication would be hindered to weaken the strong hold of the army. We ended with agreeing to disagree. The day of cafeteria church was over. I didn't want a religion but a relationship with God, the father who art in Heaven.

I later explained to my husband that I was no longer able to attend the church and pleaded with him to understand. I allowed the children to continue to go when God came to me and asked me a question. Why did I allow the children to go to a church that I couldn't go to? I fell to my knees and prayed for God to give me the strength to go against my husband and I was given the words to say. When they returned from church, I immediately took Nate in the room and told him these words. "I love you and you are my husband and I don't want you to think that I am undermining you authority. I consider your attendance at the church a job and not worship and I cannot allow Jennifer and Nate Alex to go to work with you anymore." He reaction was not that of understanding until I shared to him what God revealed to me. I asked him if he believed in tongues and he said that he did. I then asked why would he send his children somewhere to be taught differently than he believed. After that discussion we were then in agreement. Thank you God.

The children and I went nowhere; we spent all of all time at the house and park across the street. I was keeping them away from the negative influences of Nate's family. I did however try to include James children so that they could know their cousins but Rachel wanted no part of that and would often give excuses why they couldn't come over. I stopped trying.

In the later weeks, I had the urgency to dye my hair to its natural color. I then had the urgency to put tracks in the side like I wore it long ago. I spent my time playing the Sims which became my social life. Nate didn't see his family that much, but James would stop by and sit in the car for a little while to make sure he was alright. I liked James and I knew he was safe. He had a good heart and I didn't feel cautious around him.

Chapter 28

We talked about the Hurricane that was in the Gulf and that we all decided to wait it out. We talked of plans to get supplies and I was making a mental note because they knew more about Hurricanes than I did. We had evacuated twice in that year and our saving was depleted. I was late paying the electric bill and I was thinking that I must pay it or we were going to be in the dark. After James left I convinced Nate to go to Wal-Mart to shop for the Hurricane. We got water, batteries, can foods, and charcoal in case the power went out and we needed to cook all the meat in the freezer. We stored the cases of water and other supplies in the garage and went to bed after looking at the news. Hurricane Katrina was still in the Gulf.

The next morning, I turned on the TV with Mayor Naigan pleading with the people of New Orleans and Jefferson Parish to evacuate. I saw the fear on his face and I got the suit cases. I started packing the important papers and clothes that we would need to spend several days away from home. Jennifer had lost her glasses at school on Friday and I was going get them on Monday. Monday never came. We were on the road with the electric bill money and the church check. Nate went to the church to pick up his check and stated that he was evacuating and the Pastor tried to put a guilt trip on Nate but Nate knew in his spirit that God gave him good sense to know when to run and that's what we did.

There was a caravan of my family; Mike, Candace's boyfriend and the father of her second child; Sweetie Peetie and his mom; and Netty, her two girls, her son and grandson. We headed out over the Crescent city bridge passing the Dome, where the saints played football and headed East on interstate 10 towards Mississippi. We got on the twin span heading to Slidell and proceeded on interstate 20 into Hattieburg. We only stopped to gas up and use the restroom. I had packed enough food so we didn't have to purchase food on the road and we would not be lingering too long in one spot. We were headed to Dallas because it was far enough from the Gulf. We had a TV in the car and were keeping track of Katrina. We were more prepared than Netty who wanted to stop often because of this and that and it was driving me crazy. I wanted to get out of harm's way and that acted like they didn't know the severity of this storm. I wanted to leave them because Netty had a fucking attitude but my husband didn't want me to leave his sister. Mike was the man. He was on my tail and he could be my wingman always. He was running defense on the road. I would put my blinker on and he would get over first and then allow me to move over. I would scream a shout of joy because he knew what I was thinking. He had my back. Netty on the other hand got lost in the mist of the sea of cars on the road that we had to call her on the cell that we asked to borrow from her son. We did found her and we were back on track. We got caught by slow traffic and I saw dirty diapers being thrown from Netty car. How disgusting. Now that's a nigga for you. What did she care she didn't live in that city? That's the kind of attitude she had. Monkeys raised monkeys; that was my motto and it was true to form. When we finally stopped to gas and use the restroom Candace came to me and asked me did I see what they did and I just told her my motto. Monkeys raised monkeys and we both laughed. One of Netty's daughters noticed my hair that I had styled two weeks earlier. She said she always liked my hair like that and I thanked her.

We got back on the road and the news stated that there were torrential rains in Hattiesburg. We had just left Hattiesburg so I chirped all cars and told it was time to put the pedal to the metal. I told them that the storm was on our tails and I was not stopping unless it was an emergency. I was the better driver and that was okay with Nate. I was doing ninety at time to get to our destination. My feet were swollen from the unknown condition, but I told no one because I didn't want them to worry. It took us 20 hours to get to Dallas and I was a mess. I could barely walk. I damn near needed to be pried from the car seat. Every step was painful and all I wanted was a bed and my medication. We had reservations and quickly got the keys and each family went to their rooms. I got in the bed and turn on the TV. It was 6 am and Katrina was barreling down on New Orleans. It had taken out the Twin Span Bridge to get to Slidell the one we used and the Causeway. I started to freak out. Our home. I started to cry. Nate left me and went to his sister's room and that was the last time I saw him. I was in so much pain that I didn't care but I couldn't go to sleep. I laid there in the bed crying and looking at the News.

The children thought they were on vacation and that's what I wanted them to think. They kept running back and forth between rooms that were all on different floors and I told them to stay with their dad. Jennifer was 10 and Nate Alex was 8 and I was very protective and we were in a hotel filled to capacity because of the storm. I was in so much pain that I was over medicating to help endure the swollen of both feet, knees ankles and wrist. I was hooked up but Nate stayed with his sister. I was alone. I was over medicated, pissed, and abandoned. He was my husband and I didn't mind sharing but I didn't get anything. The children would knock on the door and I would have to painfully get up to open the door because he refused to give them the key so I would have to get out of bed. I ended up giving them my key to stop the arguing about him not being considerate of the way I was feeling. Fuck me! His sister needed him, even though her grown son was also with her. Candace came to see how I was doing and I had puffy eyes and a washout face. She knew I was not doing well and offered to get me breakfast and make coffee. She took care of me. I told her that this was the last straw. Governor Blanco was saying that the residents were not going to be able to go home for about 7 weeks. 7 weeks, my children just went back to school and I was supposed to be away from home for 7 weeks. How were we going to live? We used the bill money and his church check to get to Dallas stay this long. I got on the phone to call my mother to let her know that we were okay and that we were in Dallas. She told me that my brother, Jeff, wanted me to call him in Virginia. I called him and he asked me how much did I need. I told him $200 and he said that wouldn't be enough and told me he would deposit $500 in my mother's account for which I had access to. I called Jake and asked if we could come to stay with him and his wife, Marie, until we could sort things out and

Marie said that we could. I was so grateful that I was going back to California after almost 10 years of misery and abuse. I was going home. When Nate finally showed up I told him my plans. He said what about Netty. My reply was Fuck Netty. What about me and his children? I was through and I was not going to argue because I was in too much pain. The decision was made. Candace decided to come with us even though she was on again off again with Gouda's dad. I called my grandson Gouda like the cheese because of his sweaty feet and the name stuck. It was a pet name like Sweetie Peetie.

She told Mike and he didn't want to lose his sons but he knew that New Orleans was not a good place to be. I worried about him and his mom until he said he spoke to his brother and they were going to El Paso Texas to stay with them. His mother worried about his father and I thought he was working because of the Hurricane but I didn't understand why he didn't call. We thought something may have happened to him but he finally called and said he went to their home in Marrero and he was staying because the looting had begun.

We all said our goodbyes and two cars left and Netty and her family stayed at the hotel. Nate was sad and I told him he could stay with her if he wanted too but he said he was going with his family and I told him to get that pathetic look off his face as if I was making him do something he didn't want to do. I knew his M.O. and it was not going to follow me back to California. I was done. Take my ass off the grill. It was going to be a new day and I was going to be the captain of my destiny. I had sacrificed all that time for him to grow up and he looked as if he didn't change at all. I started to feel that the torture was in vain and that made me mad.

We headed towards El Paso was going to stay the night with Mike's brother and his family. I thought that was very nice of them. It appeared to me that the only bad thing about New Orleans and my experience was Nate's fucked up family. Mike's was another nice family who was considerate and they were not even church goers. No wonder why Candace did not want to go to church. All the hypocrites treated us like we were lepers, singing hymns and shouting halleluiahs. I was trying to give her a family experience and I may have caused more harm than good and for that I was deeply sorry. I did what I thought was best.

The next morning, we all said our goodbyes again and Mike cried because his sons were leaving him. He had a bond with both boys and I felt sorry for his pain but that's what happens when you drag your feet and not commit with marriage before starting a family. It would truly be a hard pill to swallow in the later years.

We all pile in the 2001 Hyundai Santa Fe and with our luggage tied to the roof of the car looking like the Beverly hillbillies. We only stopped to gas, get food and use the restroom. I wanted California and I could almost taste the sea air. I missed the beach, the weather, the mountains and the food. I had plans to kiss the ground when I got there and I was never leaving again. I'm a California girl to the bone. I was coming home and my brothers came through for me. They showed me much love. I thought maybe the 10 years away was not in vain. I felt like the prodigal child coming back to a feast. I was sorely mistaken.

Chapter 30

On August 31, 2005, we got to my brother's house and I needed another bath to soak my joints that were inflamed. I gave Marie a one hundred dollar bill and thanked her for letting us into her home. I sat for a while with my brother and had a drink of VSOP brandy. I took shots because of the Gastric bypass and my now little stomach. Soda andI didn't get along. I quickly found that VSOP was another way to dull the pain both physical and mental. My brother called my mother and I spoke with hear and Candace called her father Junior to tell him she was back. The next day we had a full house of family members wanted me to know what we had been through and I had not processed it all. Junior came in the house with his bible under his arm and I thought, is he serious? He wore his salvation like a man wanting to show he was fasting. I guess he got his blessing. He was stand offish towards my brother like he thought of Jake to be a heathen bound for Hell. I barely said two words to him. His spirit wasn't right and I felt it. His sister was also there and she was a Christian too. I was glad to see her because it had been years. She was more of a sister than my own were to me even though we had a falling out, we always forgave each other. It was a family cookout and there was food galore. I was still exhausted but I was having fun. I was home and I felt that my family came through in high style.

I put the children to bed early because life goes on and Jennifer and Nate Alex had to go back to school. I registered Jennifer in one school and Nate had to be put on a waiting list. He ended up at another school but it could be helped. Thank God I put the red box of important papers in the car before leaving New Orleans. I had everything I needed to apply for Welfare which was our next stop. I was in pain, but I had to take care of business. We all went to the Welfare office and got a not so warm welcome. We were treated horribly. We waited for an hour while being laughed at by worker pointing her finger at us and making me feel worse than I already did. I finally went to the window and asked about being seen and she told me that I didn't give her the application back. I started to argue with her, telling her misinformation is no information and that she needed better communication skills. She started to say something else and I interrupted her and asked to speak to a supervisor.

I knew the rules and nobody deserved to be treated like that. Welfare is for people in need and I was in need. I was homeless, without proper clothes for the weather and I had no food. We were known as Katrina refugees. What the fuck! I'm an American citizen; we were not refugees. The welfare agency made me feel like I was a refugee.

A Supervisor came out and things changed, Candace, Nate and I were both taken to the back to be interviewed. I had to tell them that we were separate families and I could tell Candace was getting offended. I had to let my baby bird go and this was the chance. She needed to spread her wings and be on her own. I would be there for her but she needed her own space and I needed mine. We were promised expedited services and the Supervisor was true to her word. We went to Wal-Mart and were told about Red Cross vouchers for clothes which we needed. I brought only necessities and then went to Red Cross. There, they also played dumb. They said they didn't know what I was talking about. I told them that I had summer clothes for my children and I also needed an interviewing outfit to look for work. I was told again that they didn't have anything like that. I left with the knowledge that I tried and the children began to complain that they were hungry. I went to Jack in the box to order off the dollar menu to get them something and I looked out the window at a self-serve newspaper stand. I got a paper and I went back to Red Cross. I now had visual aids. I walked into the office on fire and slammed the paper on the counter. I looked the woman in the face and told her to look. On the front page was the story of Katrina. I told her this was us and we needed help. I took my Driver's license and asked Candace and Nate for theirs. I put them on top of the paper and said "Now what? You're still going to tell me you don't know what I'm talking about?" The receptionist looked at me with no words in her mouth.

There was a representative that was there from the town of Apple Valley and she overheard the conversation. She came over to me and asked if she could talk to me. I started to cry as I told her the events over the last couple of days. I was a homeowner with two cars, a pool and trampoline in the backyard in a nice neighborhood and now I was homeless, tired and hungry, and my children were registered for school without proper clothing and Jennifer lost her glasses the Friday before that bitch Katrina came and destroyed my life. I of coursed apologized for the language because I knew she did not deserve to be spoken to in that manner but I was devastated and scared. I swore never to have to be in a position to be back on Welfare and I was. I had accomplished, by the grace of God, to purchase a home after being in New Orleans for three years and far as I knew it was gone and my husband's job was underwater. We were not on vacation. We were displaced Americans and we didn't deserve to be treated like under the table conmen who were trying to get an easy buck. I was a mess and Candace and Nate watched as I broke down. My children came to console me and I mustered enough strength to be strong for them.

A man came out of the back room and directed us to follow him. We did just that after the Apple Valley representative gave us her card and took down my brother's phone number. We were given vouchers for Target and gift cards for food at Stater Bros. Market. I was exhausted, but went to Target to get the children a few outfits for school. I also bought that interviewing outfit because I knew that I was going to have to look for work. I was grateful for Welfare, but it wasn't enough to live on.

I went back to my brother's house and was asked a million questions but I was not in the mood to talk. I was all talked out. Later, Marie and I sat for hours talking and drinking the drink that I was introduced to. It was like my own little pain killer. VSOP became my new best friend. I was glad to be home but I was constantly thinking of what will become of us.

The next morning, I received a phone call from the Apple Valley rep. who wanted to feature my family in the Daily Press newspaper. I spoke to my husband and he agreed. A journalist and a photographer came later that day. They asked a few questions and took some photos of us. It was in the paper the next day and Marie was angry that it didn't say more about her and Jake for taking us in. I paid it no mind, but I should have.

Jake asked Nate and I if we wanted to go to Las Vegas and I needed to get my mind off on my situation and so we went. Jake drove my car and Nate and I sat in the back seat. I was tired of driving so I welcomed the suggestion. Jake had complimentary coupons and so it didn't cost anything but gas and food which my brother quickly used our situation for meal tickets. I was talking while we were in the car. I was looking at all the lights when I broke out crying. They were happy tears. I was thanking Jake for coming to my rescue and I talked about how Jeff came through for me as well. I felt loved and I believe this was the first time I felt that my family had my back. Marie and Jake argued constantly on the trip and it was getting on my nerves. I tried to drown them out with my new friend but that just made me pass out. I awoke to more of the same and I tried to talk to Marie but she was one needy woman. Jake was good to her and she was never satisfied. He tried to please her in every way but still the arguing continued. Nate ended up winning on the slots and Jake began to complaining about his tags on his car needed to be renewed. I talked to Nate who agreed to pay for them. I was glad when we got back to the house. I couldn't take another minute of Marie and Jakes arguing. Candace did a fine job taking care of the children for the weekend.

The town of Apple Valley arranged for Jennifer to get new glasses and I was grateful. They also promised to pay for us to move into our own place when we found one. Nate took the car to look for work and I asked Jake for a run to the Welfare office and he complained about gas. I told him that I would put gas in his car and he told me he preferred cash so I gave him $20. I also replenished the stock of my new best friend.

Later that day we had went to the store because I wanted to barbeque. I used my food stamps to buy everything and Marie started putting things that she wanted in the basket. It wasn't a problem but I thought it was uncouth. I asked her to get whatever we needed at home and she spent over $300. That's what the money was for I guess but I started seeing a pattern. We went to Sam's Club and I wanted to thank Jake for his help so I purchased him a set of Wolfgang Puck cookware. He deserved it and I was glad I could do it. He was a good cook and needed good cookware.

I was with Jake and Marie for two weeks before the shit hit the fan. The Apple Valley rep. came to the house to present me with an envelope and I was in the back yard and Marie told her I was not there. The representative gave the envelope to Marie and she called me after the lady had left. Just enough time to open the envelope to see what was inside. I took the envelope and ran outside to catch her but she was nowhere in sight. I looked at the envelope and noticed that it had been open. Marie is really ghetto. I went back in the house and put the envelope on the counter and went back outside where the children and Jake were. I thought I would give her as much time as she needed to look at the fifteen hundred dollar check.

Jake was cooking and I stayed out of his way. He was unusually quiet and I knew something was on his mind. I had been on the phone all day and was securing two apartments for Candace and myself. The owner said she was getting them ready and I told her we would pay six months rent in advance to make the offer more attractive and she was willing to go with that. I told Jake the good news and told him that we would be out of his hair soon and he would have his house and privacy back. He told me he needed to talk to me and we went outside. He told me that he expected a little more appreciation from me and I asked him how much because I was under the impression that he took us in because we were his family. He said fuck family and that hurt. I started to cry because I was hurt that he said that and he looked me in my face and told me I could stop with the tears because they don't faze him. I told him that he better be glad I'm crying because he didn't want to see the other side. He spoke of all the money that F.e.m.a gave me and that he should get something. I asked him how what that something was and he was too shame to give me a number. He told me to give him a number and I told him already did but obviously it wasn't the number he had in mind so it was his turn and he still couldn't give me a number. Marie called for me and told me that the telephone was for me and it was Jeff who told me I should be ashamed of myself for coming to lay up on Jake. I don't lay up. It's not in my nature to lay up. I told Jeff that I should have known this was too good to be true. I was his younger sister and to be treated like a cash cow or a payday was insulting. I tried to tell Jeff that I gave Jake over $600 and that I only been here for two weeks what did they expect. I was interrupted by Pamela, Jeff wife, who said she had to pray to God to give me that money and this is the thanks they get. I told her that she was just trying to hurt me to say some shit like that. I told her to kiss my ass and hung up the phone.

Chapter 31

I told Candace and my family to get in the car. I left and went to a hotel after I stopped and bought a bottle of my new best friend. I was in shock and in disbelief of what just happened. I rented two rooms for the night one for me and one for Candace. I sat in my room dazed at the words ringing in my ears. The hatred I received from my family was unbearable. I wanted to disappear so my children couldn't see me. Nate looked as lost as me and therefore was no help. I was going in a downward spiral and I didn't know how to pull up. I was glad to be back home but at what cost? For my children to see how dysfunctional my family was too. The two families were their legacy and I was their only hope and I was losing my mind. I got myself together long enough to put Jennifer and Nate Alex to bed and then I started to drown my sorrows with VSOP. I drank until I passed out and then the words were silenced.

I woke up the next morning with a new attitude. I had to get the housing together and find another place to stay until our apartment were ready. I went back to the Welfare office and applied for Homeless assistance. I went through the ridiculousness of finding a place for 80% of the $821 of monthly aid. We were in California and rent started at $725 for a two bedroom place that would barely pass code. I was allowed the once in a lifetime assistant because I was a Katrina victim. I was a victim in many ways than one. I felt hopelessness setting in but I had to be victorious for my children who deserved better.

The rules of the Homeless program were

unreal. I had to check in every three days with a list of places that I had searched to find a place and it was impossible. I was given a voucher for a motel for drunks and frequented by prostitutes. We moved our belongings into the room and I was going to my room with Jennifer when I saw a man struggling to get into his room. I offered my assistance while I stood in front of Jennifer who insisted on poking her head around me to see the funny man and he started to sing a vulgar drunken song while looking at my baby. I pushed Jennifer back behind me and open the guy's door and grabbed Jennifer arm and hurried to our room. I sat who on the bed and laid the ground rules. I told her no shorts or tank tops and to never leave the room unescorted. Before I knew it was yelling at her and she was scared to death. When I noticed how she was looking I hugged her and began to cry saying that I was sorry. I didn't mean to scare her but I was scared myself. I couldn't have my children in such a place where men laid in the bed with their doors open and their hands down the front of their pants. I went back to the Red Cross and told them what was going on and they gave us vouchers for a decent hotel without the ridiculous limitations. The receptionist said she didn't mine giving us the vouchers because we had things. I looked at her and said, "Do you know how stupid you sound?" and walked out. Jake had to come and see how I landed on my feet and I felt sorry for him. I knew that I was going to be okay, but how he lived was his life. He was money hungry and was always looking for a fast buck. He bragged about panhandling like it was a job and that he made $200 a day begging.

We stayed at the hotel for 10 days before our apartments were ready. By this time we had purchased appliances and furniture to give it the feeling of home. I made the money stretch because Candace and I had to use all the F.e.m.a money to pay six months' rent each in advance because we were unemployed. The town of Apple Valley even tried to renege on the promise to help with the move in cost of the $725 deposit. The representative would not return my calls and it was getting close to move in date. We had no more money and needed their help because they said they would help and I used that money in the budget. I left a message that I felt like they had used the poor little Katrina victims to get publicity and that I shouldn't be surprised because my own family was milking Katrina so why shouldn't they do it too. The representative called me and set up a time to meet at the apartment to pay the deposit.

It was moved in day and I had all my ducks in a row. The furniture was delivered and by the time nightfall was here the children were taking baths to get ready for bed. By this time I was barely able to walk. The unknown condition was screaming and my knee had swelled up twice its size. Nate began to worry and I knew he couldn't do anything about it. I drank to calm my nerves and to ignore the pain that I was in. When the Medi-Cal cards came I went to a doctor who gave me cortisone shots in my knees and ankles to reduce that swelling and ease the pain and they worked wonders.

Now that Jennifer and Nate Alex was in school, I sat out to find a job. I went to the County of San Bernardino and applied for my old job back as an Eligibility Worker. I knew that job well on both sides of the desk. I got the scores back quick and was in group one. Nate got a temp job in a warehouse with crappy hours and low pay, but I was thankful, it was something. I had not heard anything from the County Human resources but I was hopeful. I had the experience and I knew that something had to come through. Even though I was going through so much I still prayed for a miracle and I knew that God hadn't forgotten me. My faith was strong but I wanted to numb my flesh to stop thinking about my family and how cruel they were. I drank every night after the children went to bed to stop thinking of the horrible things that were said to me.

We later got a letter that we were eligible for Section 8, the rent assistance program, and I was thankful but I also wanted a job and God heard my prayer. I was offered the job for the County of San Bernardino. Now Nate and I were going to be working. Things were looking up but we were no longer going to be eligible for Section 8. No problem. God had provided us both with jobs and we were going to be okay.

In the meantime, Nate and I had to trek back to New Orleans on the greyhound bus to tie up affairs dealing with the house and the car we had to leave behind. The car had to be repaired from all the debris that hit it in the storm but the house was untouched. Nate and I walked around the house amazed that we had only minor dings in the siding but the roof was still intact even though the houses on both sides received damage. I started praising the Lord for his mercy and grace. We stayed in the house while we packed up our personal belongings and had a garage sale for the furniture and appliances. We then used the money to ship our things back to California with the money we made. I sold the stuff for cheap because we were all hurting and the people who stayed needed help. We had furniture and all our necessities in California and couldn't, even if we wanted to, take too much stuff back. I paid our neighbor across the street for keeping the grass cut to show my appreciation. We were there for a week and no one invited us to dinner and then had nerve to act sad when it was time for us to go.

F.e.m.a paid for me to fly back home and Nate drove his car back. I worried about him, but he was a man and could do it. I knew he could. Candace met me at Ontario airport and was late as usual. I was irritable and she thought I was mad at her. I was too tired to convince her otherwise. I thanked her for keeping the kids and told her that I needed a bath and a bed and went to my apartment. The things that we shipped were already at the bus depot in Victorville and I would take care of it tomorrow. I was tired but I could not sleep. I was so sleepy that I could not think and I rested in the bed for days until Nate arrived home with the car.

He took one look at me and knew I needed to go back to the doctor. We found out that I had mixed connective tissue disorder where my white cell attacked my joints causing swelling and severe pain. I now had a name for what's been ailing me. I was relieved even though I was still in pain. Just to know what it was brought me some comfort. I got more cortisone shots to give me relief and I was off and running again.

It was five months since Katrina and I was

now in training. I had to go forty-five miles one way for training. Gas was not cheap and the Employment service program offered me 2 $15 gas card to make it there for six weeks. I had to let bills go unpaid so I could have gas to make the trip. I dared not ask a family member for money. One day at lunch time I got a flat tire and I had no money to get a new one and it could not be repaired. I called my mother and told her my dilemma. She reluctantly agreed to let me get the money out of her bank account to buy a new tire and then took my name off of her account.

Ouch, that hurt.

I even left a hundred dollars in her bank when Jeff gave me the money, so really she didn't give me anything but that was my family.

After training, I got a position in the High Desert which was a Godsend. I was in Adelanto for three months and then I started feeling ill. It felt like I was having a heart attack. On Sunday, I told Nate I needed to go to the hospital because I was not feeling well. I had had an anxiety attack and it felt like I had an anvil sitting on my chest. I was hooked to the monitor and everything came up clean. The doctor asked me about my life and I just broke out crying. What life? I couldn't see my future. I felt alone and he asked me if I thought about killing myself. I told him often but my life was not mine to take. Jennifer heard me and I repeated my life is not mine to take then smiled at her and she seemed relieved. I was given Valium then sent home and told to follow up with my primary care doctor. I lost thirty pounds in many days. I couldn't eat, I couldn't sleep and I couldn't think. I went to work and had a nervous breakdown. I froze at the computer after talking to my supervisor about not doing well. I couldn't remember the computer system functions and I felt stupid. I usually learned very quickly but I was having a major brain fart. I couldn't retain any information and I told my supervisor I quit. He asked for my badge after seeing that he could not convince me that everything would be alright. I grabbed my things and shamefully worked out of the office. I got to my car that I had just purchased and cried like a baby. I was alone and scared. What was I going to tell Nate who depended on my income for provision. I handled the finances and I began to resent him for making me responsible for everything. I felt that if he would have helped me then I wouldn't have lost it. I started the car and drove, crying all the way home to the now three bedroom home that we couldn't afford and driving the car I wouldn't have a way to pay for. Yes, we had sold the house in Louisiana at a 40,000 lost in inequity since Katrina. I felt robbed and I wanted to know why. I prayed to come back to California, but not like this. The pain was too great and I felt as if I was losing my mind. I thought for a minute about ending it all but remembered that my life was not mine to take. I cried out to God but I felt alone. I was alone.

Nate came home from work and I told him what I had done. I cried as I told him that I couldn't think, that I could see my future and that I was scared. Nate had no facial expression that I could read, but I knew he was disappointed in me and I felt hopeless. I stayed in the bedroom crying and whenever the children came into the room I would stop and wipe my tears because I didn't want to scare them.

The next morning, when the kids went to school and Nate went to work I got dressed and went to the Department of Behavior Health. I knew something was wrong, but I didn't know what it was. I was diagnosed with Post Traumatic Stress Disorder and begin taking Prozac. I started going to therapy and I would cry while asking the same question. What was wrong? I had always been strong and I questioned my faith in myself. I had let myself down. How could I be so weak? I've been through much more than Katrina and she brought me back to California. I felt guilty because I was home and it was making my family suffer. My desires made my family suffer. A lot of people died so I could come home. We didn't have money to pay our monthly expenses. We went from buying and living in a beautiful home to renting a home that rented for more that our mortgage and on top of that we had to sell our house at a loss to prevent foreclosure.

I wondered what I had done to deserve such punishment. Was it because I touched God's anointed Pastor in New Orleans, the Baptist Minister that denounced speaking in tongues? No it couldn't be. I was defending a gift of God. I was a child of God and he loved me. After therapy I would go home and prepared a nice meal for my family but I could not eat. I continued to take the Prozac and prayed for God to get me out of this pit that I had somehow gotten myself into.

My family was not there for me, Candace thought I had lost my mind and I felt that I let Nate down and he had damaged goods. I had no value at all and I was the special one. I prayed for Grace and mercy, for forgiveness for my unbelief.   I felt like I was in the belly of the whale and didn't know what I had done to get there. I cried out and still I felt that it was on deaf ears. Lord, what did I do to be in this state? I tried to do the right thing. Sure, I had sin, but no greater than others who were having a more abundant life. I had desires and dreams of success with the ability to help others that were less fortunate than me. I heard complaints about being rude. I wasn't rude; I was honest to people that I knew and who I thought knew me. I kept my mouth shut when my advice was not being taken and I always helped where and when I could. Okay, I would like to hear that people did learn a lesson and yes I didn't help again when they made the same mistake twice. Like Charles taught me, the first time you bump you head on the brick wall it was a learning tool, but if you do it again you should consider yourself stupid. A one way ticket to Dumbdom. Dumbdom is a city where irresponsible people who don't want to suffer the consequences of their actions live.

Chapter 32

Nate Alex was doing poorly in school and I told Nate to take his television out of his room. Nate was slow about doing everything and I felt that that was why Nate Alex didn't care about doing well in school. I was not going to let my son fall through the cracks as my husband had apparently fallen through already. I had to get my son away from the mentality that had plagued my husband and he was of no help to me anyway. I carried all of the burden and he just added to the pressure with his passive aggressive attitude. I was tired and scared and I felt that Nate was an anchor around my neck. I knew that I was not getting better and I didn't want to get back on welfare with him. I felt as if I was drowning. I went to Nate Alex room and began to remove the television when Nate had come in behind me not to take it. He grabbed me and I socked him in his face. He held me tight so I couldn't hit him again. Jennifer and Nate Alex ran to the hall and the phone started to ring. I broke loose from his grip and ran to the bedroom and took the money I had withdrawn out of the bank while I answered the phone. It was Candace. She asked me why I was breathing hard and I told her I couldn't take it anymore and that I had to go. I hung up the phone and told the children to get in the car. They did what they were told and I drove to a hotel and checked in. I called Candace and told her that I was alright and that I would see her in the morning. I put the children to bed and lied down for hours thinking of what next.

The next morning, I went back to the house and took our clothes and went to Candace house. I checked the children out of school and registered them in the schools in Candace's district. I figured that the money was mine since I paid Nate's car off to the tune of $7000. Unconscientiously, I knew I was going to leave him and that event was the last straw. I felt trapped and I couldn't see my future. I needed time and space away from Nate and to figure what I wanted in my life, but the decision was made for me by two men that I once loved.

I had planned on helping Nate moved to an apartment that he could afford on his own and give him all the furniture and when I saw that he was taking responsibility I would take him back. I told Candace not to tell her father that I had left Nate and was now living with her but she did and he was up in Apple Valley in a quickness to fix her brakes on her car. I spoke to him, but stayed in the room because I knew I was in a vulnerable state. Nate had come over to get the children and he saw that Junior/Pot was there. He changed his name supposedly for pottery clay as in Christian to be molded by God or some shit he was talking and I fell for it hook line and sinker. He began calling every day and we spoke often about the Bible and scriptures. We also talked about my plans for the future. At that time, I had none. I was waiting for a sign so to speak. I had no job, I was newly separated and I had two children.

I applied for Welfare again and this time Nate was not on the case. A social worker came out to see the living arrangements while I was getting the children ready for school. It was a quick visit but she had gotten all the information needed to have the worker process the case. I then changed my bank account to take Nate's name off of my account and me off of his. The bank made a mistake and sent my checks to the wrong apartment in the quadplex and the occupants took my checks and cashed them at five stores. I went to the bank and discovered that I was $200 overdrawn. I had to file a police report and even with video footage at one of the stores, the girl got away with the crime. I was told that I couldn't press charges because the bank gave me back my money and the bank refused to press charges. She got away with it and then had the audacity to continue to borrow household products from my daughter as if she was vindicated.

I tried to talk to Candace but she thought she was doing the Christian thing and I saw betrayal. I allowed it until she came to borrow toilet paper twice in the same week while throwing Mickey beer bottles all over the courtyard. I told Candace how I felt and she understood. I put a sign on the door that read:

"*The market and Dollar store is down the street and the Bank is on the corner. This is not it. Please do not ask to borrow again.*"

That stopped a lot of knocks on the door.

I attended a program for the Welfare to get a job and I liked the classes but was kicked out when my case was denied. I spoke to my worker who told me that it was a mistake and that the benefits will be put on the card the next day. I asked about the class and was told that someone from the program will be calling me soon.

As I waited for a call, Pot called and came to see me. He would take me to lunch and we would talk about old times and the mistakes we made. I began to see the changes in him and in my mind I thought that maybe he was delivered from his old ways. Nate barely spoke to me while Pot gave me lots of attention. After two weeks of the butter up, the shit hit the fan.

The owner of the house called about the pool and barbeque pit that was left. I called Nate to get help removing the items and he told me that I had a man let do it. I told Nate that he was my husband and that nothing was going on and it wasn't but Nate was not hearing me and hung up in my face. I was devastated and I felt angry and abandoned. I cried from the pain of feeling betrayed yet again by the man that claimed to love me. I soon allowed a huge monkey to get on my back. I called Pot who was happy to take care of it. He was there in a hurry and on time. He moved the pool alone and would not let me help. The feeling felt great. I felt like a lady. He treated me so fragile and I had forgot what that felt like being with Nate who depended on me for everything. I moved the furniture and cooked the food. With Pot it was different. I felt like I had a man who let me be a lady and I savored the moment. During the move he told me that he wanted to take me out. I was surprised and happy at the same time. We made plans and it was a date. Pot then took the pool and pit to Candace's garage all without my help and he had to keep telling me to get out of his way. I loved the quality of a man that didn't need my help. It was attractive. He had the control and I was able to not think of how, when what and where. It felt like I was being taken care of instead of me taking care of someone.

Friday had come and Nate came to get his children and he thought he was hurting me but that gave me the opportunity to be free. I got dressed and headed down the 15 freeway listening to Beyonce, Janet, and Fergie. I had black jeans with heels, a sexy blouse that showed a modest amount of cleavage and my leather jacket. My hair was a curly free flowing brown wig with golden highlights. I was the skinniest I had ever been because I was stressed by the break up and I used it to my advantage.

When I arrived, Pot gave me the once over and by his look he was pleased. I never received looks like that from Nate and it felt good. I had lost over one hundred and twenty five pounds five years ago and I felt sexy for the first time in my life. I felt free. Pot took me to a southern restaurant and I had ribs and potato salad for which I couldn't finish and had to get a to-go box. That just made me felt more attractive. Pot was impressed that I didn't eat it all and he commented that I looked swank. I asked for clarification and he told me classy. He laid it on thick and I lapped it up like a thirsty puppy in a puppy mill. I was on cloud nine and I had the thought of seduction. Nate did said let my man do it and he was acting like my man.

He drove my car from the restaurant while we listened to Heather Headley. I enjoyed the way that he took control and my loins began to ache. I could feel myself getting moist and I kept squirming in the passenger seat. I had not felt this in years and I was excited. I don't know what movie we saw because that was not where my mind was. I was deep in thought about having sex; real sex that I had been missing since I got married some thirteen years ago. I endured the mediocre sex with Nate hoping for it to come back like when we were fornicating but it never did. I told Pot my intentions and he acted surprise. I told him to feel my crotch and he was surprised at how wet I was. I took his hand and shoved it down the front of my skinny jeans and he let out a gasp of delight. He played with my clitoris and I moaned in ecstasy. I was ripe for the picking and I ask that he take me back to his place. I popped the Janet Jackson CD into the player to indicate my intentions. I was going to get laid tonight and I was not taking no for an answer.

We got back to Pot's apartment that was dark and gloomy but I didn't care. I had my mind on other things like letting him take care of it. I sat on his bed and he sat on a chair across the room. I asked why he was so far and motioned him to sit next to me on the bed. He hesitated then finally complied. I told him that I had been deprived for so long and that I couldn't contain myself. At first Pot refused which made me want him all the more. He had gained some weigh but it was all muscle and hard. I held on to his arm and noticed the scar that I had put there more than twenty five years ago. I kissed it and told him that that should never have happened. I told him that I still loved him and that I knew he felt the same about me. I told him that this was his chance and the ball was in his court. I tried to kiss him and he resisted but I refused to chase him. I knew about the hunt and I was going to make him beg for me. I lied on his bed and told him that he had something on his face. When his hand went to his face my scent went up his nose and he pounced on me. He had not washed his hand and my juices had dried on his hand and boy was it sweet.

We started to kiss and before long the clothes were off. I had the time of my life and I thought thank you Jesus. I was in the grave with several monkeys on her back. I felt that God would forgive me and that I had waited long enough. I was deprived, angry, hurt and I felt abandon by Nate and I was going to have pleasure and I did. I stayed the night but I didn't sleep very well. I toss and turned because I couldn't sleep and I wanted to make up for lost time. I was like a ravenous dog wanting more kibbles and bits. Pots wanted to sleep and I told him that I could sleep at home and got up and left. I drove home at 3 am listening to Fergie, Janet, and Beyonce. I got my fix and was ready to go home to Candace apartment and get the sleep I needed. Every weekend Pot and I were together. He even invited me to go bowling with his employees to show me off. I didn't mine because I did look hot. The guys were looking at me like damn! I was flattered and tickled and Pots was proud. One of the guys said something inappropriate and Pots blasted him for it. How attractive I thought. I remembered the time that Nate allowed his coworker to undress me with his words and said nothing. Pots looked like he was ready to take this man's head off. I felt love and protected. Finally a man that was not afraid to defend his woman.

He was no punk, I tell you that.

Jennifer called and I told her that I was at the bowling alley and she wished she was there. I told her that I would take her one day. She asked me when I was coming home and I told her I would be there before she woke up in the morning. She started to cry and say she wanted me now but it was impossible because I was in Anaheim which was more than 70 miles away. Those monkeys were piled high on my back and I didn't know it. My baby wanted her mother and I was being free and single with my other daughters' father. I was deep in the grave.

I managed to make it home before the children woke up and my tank was full. I took a bath to remove any scent that I didn't want my children to smell rather it be cologne or other things. Candace was upset but she said nothing and neither did I. I thought I was giving her what she always wanted: her father. I had no idea that I was destroying our relationship in the process. I had skills and he was like a dog in heat. When he was not able to see me, Pot would call and we would talk for hours late at night when the children were sleep. He knew the times that my children were home and was not to call to interrupt their time with me. He also knew their bed time. I thought I had kept the relationship under wraps until Jennifer asked me if I was having sex with Pot. She asked me while I was driving and I stared straight ahead so I wouldn't lose control of the car. I asked her what made her ask me such a thing and she said her daddy told her. I was livid. That son of a bitch involved my baby into this bullshit. How could he hurt her? I calmed myself to speak in a low tone so she would not detect my anger. I answered her question then begin to explain why. I told her I felt abandon by daddy and that I tried to figure things out but daddy was being mean and then I told her about the pool incident. I never wanted to be having this conversation with my baby but I was forced.

I felt bad, but not as mad as I felt at Nate for his bitch ass move. What was he thinking? Didn't he care about his daughter or was he like other men that only thought of themselves? The cat was out of the bag and Thanksgiving was coming. Candace had asked me to go to Arizona with her to visit Pots son, her half-brother by Naïve and now I had decided to go. This would be the first holiday that I would be away from my children and I was so angry that I used it as a way to go. Pot and I drove in his truck and Candace drove my car. We met Marquis and Candace was glad to see her brother after seventeen years. Candace had been thinking of her brother and wondered how he was doing. I knew Naive was in Alabama so I did some research and got the number and called her. I gave her the information to give to Marquis and he called back. I saw how happy Candace was and I felt good while I was not thinking of Jennifer and Nate Alex. They seemed fine, they were with their dad every weekend and I was drinking like a fish and masking my pain. Jennifer came to me and said that I looked happy and that's all the mattered to her while Nate Alex didn't care.

Chapter 33

In Arizona, Pot and I got a room at a hotel while Candace and her children stayed with Marquis and his family. Pot wanted a smoking room and I thought that to be strange since he didn't smoke. I later found that he didn't smoke tobacco. We went to the car and I smoked a cigarette while he came out with a pipe and a film container. I had no idea that he smoked pot. This Christian man was doing drugs and I had told him my testimony about my drug deliverance. I was shocked. I thought fornication was an affair of the heart but drug use was definitely a no no. I said nothing but it got me to thinking. What else is there to see? We got up the next morning and headed back over to Marquis's apartment. We brought breakfast because we weren't sure of what we would find to eat. It was Thanksgiving Day and Pot was a little standoffish. Marquis had others for dinner and I was talking to everyone. Later that day Pot went outside and cried because he said he never thought he would ever spend a holiday with both his children. I felt for him and told him to go and be with them and enjoy the moment. He told me he needed a little time to get his self together and I excused myself and went back in the apartment. Pot came in a little time later and it appeared that he had gotten his self together and the evening resumed. All the guests had left and we began to drink and play scrabble. The children had been put to bed and we got a little tipsy. I got a lot tipsy. My children were not with me but I did miss them. I wished that they were with me but I knew that was impossible so I drank. Pots and his children began making fun of me being drunk and Candace took a picture of me. They were laughing and I didn't find anything funny. I started to feel sad until the tears came streaming down my face. Candace apologized while she still laughed and that hurt me even more. I went outside and began to take a walk in the middle of nowhere in Arizona in the night. I was hurt and no one was defending me now. They were talking about how funny I looked and it made me think of the Bell Palsy. The monkey on my back. Memories of Pots and how he used to say I looked mentally challenged. Candace came after me and I cried uncontrollably. She asked me what was wrong and I told her that my feelings were hurt. I thought she had my back but I felt that she had her brother and father and she didn't need me anymore. That monkey was riding bare back. All my insecurities had surfaced and I felt so vulnerable. Candace went back to the apartment and told Pots, her father, to go and talk to me. He came and calmed me down and I went back into the apartment but I had nothing to say. I didn't want to play scrabble anymore and I was tired when Pots said it was time to go. I sat there when he asked me if I was ready and I sat for a few seconds contemplated if I wanted to go anywhere with him. I finally made the decision to go. We got to his truck and he asked why was I tripping. I turned back around and went back to Marquis' apartment while he trailed me asking where was I going and to get in the truck. I turned and told him to fuck himself. Candace opened the door and I asked Marquis if I could stay with them and he said it was alright. Pots ended up driving back to California that night because he expected me to pay for the room that night. I started seeing signs of the old Junior but I wasn't yet convinced.

Candace, I and my grandchildren went shopping for early Christmas presents at the mall then we headed back to California. We talked on the way home and I told her that I think I was making a mistake. She didn't say much except for me to follow my heart. My heart didn't want to be a single parent; my heart didn't want to be alone with all this sagging skin from all the weight loss; my heart had no job and was on Welfare and I felt that my husband gave me to another man and didn't fight for me.

We made it back home and Jennifer and Nate Alex came home a couple of hours later. It was my weekend because Nate had them for the holidays. I told them how much I missed them and I couldn't stop kissing them. I felt that my family was broken and I had no way of repairing it. I had gone too far.

Pot called Candace and ignored me for the incident in Arizona and the monkeys on my back made me believe that I had messed up. I became lonely and withdrawn, but Candace milked the situation because now her father was calling her more and I was out of the picture. She seemed happy at my expense and I stepped back for her benefit even though it hurt. I pretended like it didn't matter and I found solace in the bottle. My life was a wreck and I had no idea of how to get out of it. I missed Nate, but I also missed the attention that Pot offered me. I felt like a woman, a sexy woman, but now I was reduced to being only a mother and I gave all my attention to my children. Nate was angry because I had confessed to him that

I had sex with Pot and he felt that I had ruined our family. Candace invited me to Pot's church and we went to Sunday school. The teacher was Pot. He was so educational and he spoke of the love Jesus has for us and I was in awe. I knew what he had done with the fornication and with the drug use but I saw an anointing in him. He was almost in tears when he spoke of the goodness of Christ and I felt that God himself was speaking to me. Nate came in my mind as a pacifier until God did his work on Pot and with my help he would begin to live for Jesus and to fulfill Gods will. In my mind, Jesus gave us grace and mercy and it was extended to us even in all the sin that we had committed. After the service I spoke to him and told him that he did an amazing job. That day we forgave each other and thought to try again.

It was December 12, 2006, Candace's birthday and I told Nate that we were going to Pot's church and in morning worship he brought the children. Pot Candace and I sat together while Nate, Jennifer and Nate Alex sat on the side lines that was considered the overflow. I saw them and was happy they were there and I felt no guilt because I felt that the Lord had been pleased with me and gave me the man that I desired. He delivered Pot from his former self of abuse and promiscuity. I had a whole habitat of monkeys on my back and I didn't know it. Nate was fuming and Jennifer did all she could to keep him calm. Pot sat in his seat squirming as well and I told him that everything was alright. I was so lost and couldn't see a thing that was plain as the nose on my face.

Before the service was over, Pot had left and Candace and I didn't know where he had gone.

After service I spoke to Nate and the children and I gave them kisses. Jennifer and Nate Alex wanted to go with me but I told them that I thought it best that they stayed with their dad. I knew that Nate was hurting but I felt that our season was over and he did give me to Pot. I felt that God had made things right and after thirteen years of drought and longsuffering I had paid the price for happiness. I so wanted to be desired, respected and adored and I felt that after all the years Pot finally saw that I was a good woman worthy to be a Christian man's wife. I felt that Nate was a musician and from his actions he only went to church to play music. I became enamored by Pot's knowledge of scripture. I wanted to learn more about the word like he had taught me to drive a stick shift, do laundry, speak better and understand business. We would have our own bible study then we would make love. I was in the dark but I was deceived by my fleshly desires. I wanted to be closer to God and Nate. We never talked about the bible. He never could discuss with me the sermons that we would hear after we left church service. I would often ask him if he was even there. Pot on the other hand would speak with such zeal that it made me excited and we would talk for hours. I would ask him a question and he knew where to find a scripture that I was talking about and I knew that God had finally given me a Christian in Pot.

I finally found Pot walking on the church grounds and he was upset. I asked him what was wrong and he said he felt uncomfortable that Nate and the children were there. I asked him why did it matter as long as they got good word. I never knew that the guilt that Pot felt was his deception, not yet anyway. I was able to calm him down and we went to breakfast. By this time Nate and the children had left and I told Pot not to ruin Candace's birthday. We went to a restaurant and a cartoonist was there and he drew a likeness of me bowling the wrong way. I thought it was cute and I showed Pot. He laughed and then we went to his apartment and changed our clothes and went bowling. I was bowling the right way, but I had no idea that my life was going in the wrong direction. I thought I had things figured out. The monkeys had convinced me that the life I had was over and a new one was about to take off. How wrong I was. After we finished bowling, we went back to Pot's apartment and played scrabble which was my favorite game. I started to drink liquor and we were having a good time. Candace had left the room and Pot knowing that I was already inebriated gave me another drink and told me if I love him that I would take the drink. I was shocked and hurt that he would say something like that to me. I took it because I wanted to dull my pain. I knew Candace would protect me so I didn't care anymore. I felt that I was in a lose-lose situation. I had hurt Nate beyond measure and I was with a man that knew the bible and I couldn't help but feel that he was trying to take advantage of me.

I was not fit to drive and Candace had to bring us home. I felt like the dummy I was. Thank God my grandchildren were asleep. When we got home, Candace had to get me and the children out of the car. My life was going downhill and I was not being a role model to Candace I was a pathetic drunk.

Chapter 34

The next morning, I was ashamed and embarrassed. I had nothing to say and I felt horrible. I had disgraced myself, my family, my children, and Nate. I said that I didn't feel well and I didn't but it was not physical it was mental and spiritual. My convictions were getting to me and all I wanted to do was drown my pain with my best friend VSOP.

A week went by and I was still in a stank mood when I got a call from my dear friend Sandra. She wanted to come up from Colton which was about thirty miles away. Candace thought it would get me out of my mood before Mike, Gouda's father came from New Orleans. She planned a party and that got my mind out of the guilt that I felt. We invited family and friends, including Nate, and Pot was going to get Mike from the Airport at LAX. I had planned for Nate and the children to be long gone before Mike and Pot was due to arrive. Now I had put two monkey of secrets on my back. I was dressed in a red halter dress with four inch sling back strap sandals and I smelled fabulous and looked it. I gave Sandra another red dress that I had and we were gorgeous. I drank at the party but not to the extent of being drunk. I didn't want my children to see me as nothing but mom. I danced with Nate and I wished that we could work out our differences, but he was too shy and it was hindering his speech and it wasn't attractive. I wanted him, no, needed him, to speak up for me but he said nothing even after Jake, who was at the party, said that it was a shame that Nate was getting me all worked up for another man. A comment that I didn't hear myself, but I was told later that it was said.

The Christmas party was coming to an end, because I knew that Mike's plane had landed and I knew too well how Pot drove because he taught me. I tried to rush Nate and the children to go to his place because I didn't want them to see one another. Nate was lingering around and I was becoming agitated. He was always slow and this was no exception. Finally, I said in a harsh tone for him to leave now. He gave me a stare that tore through me and all I wanted was another drink. I wanted to mask my shame and the fact that I was excited about seeing Pot. Sandra, Candace and I sat talking about the party and the things that went on like Sandra being fed Jell-O shooters by Marie's gay daughter. I told Sandra that I didn't know she swung that way but I still loved her as long as she didn't try that crap with me. We laughed because Marie's son was also after Sandra.

Mike and Pot finally arrived at the apartment and we played dance revolution and drank some more. We finally were so drunk that we decided it was time to go to bed. I invited Pot to the bed that both Jennifer and I shared. I had an ugly monkey on my back, but the alcohol kept it hidden from me.

While in the bedroom, I took a cat nap while Pot went to take a shower and I woke up went he entered the room. We started to make out and then we started to have sex. He asked me to slap him and I obliged. He asked me to hit him harder and I obliged and as I hit him, I could feel him growing inside of me. I knew that something was not right with this man, then I got my senses. I told him that I didn't want to hurt him and that he deserved better. He told me if I didn't hit him, he was going to sock the shit out of me. I told him that if he did, I would fuck him up. Pot then called me a bitch and I was appalled and couldn't understand where this was coming from. He called me another woman's name and I wanted to escape. I got so angry that I started to call him Nate and all I wanted was Nate. Pot began to get vulgar and I told him that I was not that drunk that I wouldn't remember everything in the morning and I pushed him off of me. I felt violated and dirty. I wanted to disappear, but sleep over came me and I was out.

I woke the next morning and put on my robe. I went to the bathroom and found that my clothing was on the floor. Did I walk to the bedroom in the nude with Mike in the house? I was livid and scared of what I might have done. My only solace was that Candace was there and I knew she would not let me go too far. I washed my face and went in the living room where Sandra slept. She was already awake and said she needed to talk to me. I was scared that she would tell me I did something outrageous. She proceeded to tell me that after I went into the bedroom and Pot finished his shower, he came to her naked with a towel covering only his member stating that if he wasn't with me that he would be with her. I believed her and knew at that point that he had not changed and I was truly deceived. I sat there digesting the information and figured out a plan of what to do next. I knew he had to go. He had to get out of my life and that my children would not be safe with him. I believe in second chances but the writing was on the wall in bold letters and I was not a dummy. God was trying to tell me something and I wouldn't listen, but it was if he had to use a bull horn to tell me to let go and let go is what I did.

I went to the room and Pot was pretending to be sleep. I told him to wake up and he didn't move. I finally shook him to wake him. He acted it out to the hilt. Startled, yawning and stretching and I told him to give me a break. I told him that I had introduced Sandra as my sister friend of twenty years and obviously that meant nothing to him. He blamed whatever he did on the liquor, it was always the liquor and I told him that he needed to quit drinking because he was nasty. I talked about the events that happened last night and he claimed that he didn't remember that either and I told him it didn't matter because I did.

Candace and Mike were still in the room and I wanted him gone before they left to go Christmas shopping. I didn't want them to leave and Pot is still in the apartment. I did want to tell Candace what had happened, but I said nothing. Pot went in the bathroom and I told Sandra that if he tried anything that I was going to go for what I knew. We sat in the living room talking about the nights events and I asked her if she saw me walking through the apartment naked because all my clothing from the night before was on the floor in the bathroom including my panties and bra. Sandra said she didn't see anything but that she heard the slapping. I became embarrassed and I told her that I slapped the shit out of him and he liked it. I told her that was some scary shit because I knew I didn't want to get hit. I had been there and done that and it was not my kind of party and we both broke out laughing. Pot finally came out of the bathroom and got his things and left and I locked the door behind him.

When Candace returned, I took her in the room and told her what happened. She was disappointed and hurt and I told her that I was sorry. She was more concerned about me and I told her I was fine but I wasn't. I had made a huge error in judgment and I was going to have to go through something that I couldn't imagine.

I sunk deeper into the bottle and I didn't care if Pot cared or not. That definitely was not my life and the life of my children. My children could not be around someone with a lust spirit and that man had several. I would be devastated if something were to happen to them because my lapse in judgment. I thank God for the revelation and asked for forgiveness of my behavior. I threw my morals out the window and God brought to me that I was sleeping with the devil and I refused to listen but he saved me anyway. I was back in the city of Dumbdom, you know where irresponsible people lived, but I felt the God protected me.

I started to reflect on my life. What to do next? I had to make a plan and when I got a letter from the Welfare office about a new Job club class I was ready to go. I needed to get to work and the job was not just going to fall into my lap. I was successful in the class and was told that I would have gotten the job in a mock interview. I was even told that I would be good at the Job of an Employment Service Specialist and I was honored so much that I applied for the job. I also applied for child support officer and juvenile probation. I was taking a test every week for County employment. I went to Job fairs. I even applied for Target and was told that they didn't have a position that suited my qualification. I was a head baker a Super Wal-Mart in New Orleans before Katrina. What were they talking about? I knew something had to be wrong. I applied again and again I got another postcard saying my services were not needed at this time. I felt devalued and hopeless. Then I met an older man who wanted to get me a job but I was not interested in a pyramid scheme. I had too much sense for that. I also was not interested in giving him the Hope diamond however I did let him taste it. No not that! He touched it and then licked him finger and said I smelled sweet. I was grossed out and didn't want to talk to him anymore plus Candace said he looked dead anyway.

It was time to get out of the grave and I had to go to God for assistance. I had tried it my way and clearly it was not working. I had messed up royally and I had no idea what to do. One afternoon, I went to Wal-Mart to pick up some necessities and this man was selling CD of gospel music. I turned him down because I couldn't stand peddlers.

Chapter 35

Candace was getting tired of me being at her apartment and wanted her space and my children were getting antsy. I told Nate I was ready to come home because I had made a mess of my life and I wanted stability for the children and myself. He accepted me with open arms, and Candace and her children celebrated when I left. I went back to the apartment because I'd forgotten something and they were jumping all over the furniture like the munchkins from the Wizard of Oz when the house fell on the wicked witch. I was hurt and I told Candace that the respect she show me was the respect she would get from her children and left.

I kept the children in Candace's district and went back to a small 2 bedroom apartment and I was trying to be happy. I cooked and cleaned and made sure he had dinner. I had not yet gotten a job and I was still depressed. I looked to God for guidance and I felt that I had done so much wrong that God was not hearing me. Nate accepted me back, but the relationship had not changed. I continued to drink to endure my pain and would often be drunk in order for him to touch me. We had no intimacy and there was no communication.

Jennifer met a friend at the apartment and they quickly got close. The child lived with her father and two other siblings. She reminded me of myself and I wanted to help her. I took her shopping and treated her with kid gloves. I saw that she needed love and I was the one to give it to her like my friends mother who gave me the bra. Her father was a different story. He was a hood rat who would often say inappropriate things to me and I had to show her that I was from the streets just not of the streets. I guess Nate had told him his sob story of my infidelity and he thought that he would be next in line. Boy, was he wrong. I quickly put a stop to his expectations but monkeys will be monkeys.

One day he propositioned me and I told him I knew what Nate did to me but why would he want to hurt my husband. He didn't know what to say. I just walked away from him feeling insulted. Jennifer and Nate Alex seemed okay and I told Jennifer that she was not allowed in her friend's home. She didn't understand but she obeyed me but I kept an eye on her just in case. Nate Alex had it harder. He was often alone and his dad didn't spend much time with him. The kids would call him retard or gay depending on the day. Nate Alex was neither. He was just a kid that was not put into grown situations and had a true child's mind. Both Jennifer and Nate Alex were children and I was eager and I fought to keep their innocence. Every day, I would take the children to Apple Valley to their school and come back home. When the gas got low I would stop by Candace apartment until they were out of school. One day, after a while, I went to Candace's apartment and I could smell this awful smell coming from inside her unit. When I opened the door I was shocked. Every room in the apartment was a mess. I went from room to room to clean. Her kitchen had thawed out meat that had sat for days and was rotting. I knew my baby needed help and a mother's love was priceless. After cleaning the kitchen I put Red Beans in a crock pot and continue with the rest of the apartment. I did laundry and threw many bags of trash into the dumpster. The rice was the last thing that I did before going to get my children from school. I wrote Candace a note that read:

Taking out the trash	$5.00
Cleaning the bathroom	$10.00
Cleaning the bedrooms	$20.00
Doing the laundry	$30.00
Cleaning the kitchen $100.00	
Making a nice dinner	$10.00
A mother's love Priceless.	

I left the note on the dining room table and locked the door behind me. Candace called me later crying and I told her that I was there for her. I told her not to be afraid to ask for help if she needed it but the apartment was too messed up. I asked her if she was depressed and she stated that she just had a lot on her plate. I told her that I didn't want my grandchildren living in such conditions and that if she was over her head, she would have to let something go but mother hood was not an option. Candace agreed, but she didn't, she continued to make excuses and I continued to resent her because I was taking care of two homes both where I felt unappreciated. This was not my life.

One day Marie and Candace came to visit me and I was listening to music and visiting with my best friend VSOP. Nate came home from work and I asked him how his day was. He said fine as usual and greeted Candace and Marie and excused himself to get cleaned up. He never came back out of the room and they were there for a while. Marie commented the Nate barely said two words to me and I told her that's the way it was.

Candace had gone to New Orleans and Mike proposed to her. He had made plan to come down in April to married her and then go back home to finish his program for Electrical Engineer. I was happy for her and told her not to make the same mistakes I made as I took another sip of my friend. They soon left and I served Nate dinner and went in the room and took a sleeping pill. I was miserable, lonely, and in pain. This was not my life.

Candace called and told us the date of the wedding to take place in Las Vegas. We made reservation and she bought me a wig that made me look older than I was. It was her wedding and I didn't want her to think I was jealous so I went along with her wishes. It was, after all, her day. She told Nate that she wanted both of her father's to give her away and Nate went along with it but Pot declined but came to see her get married.

April 28, 2008, the wedding date of Candace and Mike. We got to Vegas on Friday the 27th and fed the children and then went to see some sights. It was late and Nate was tired and he stayed in the room with the children while Candace and I went to find my mother.

My cell phone rang and it was Pot. I told him we were in the lobby and he told me to come to his room. I told him that we will be up there and to give me his room number and he asked me who was "we". I told him Candace and me. He refused to give me the room number and I hung the phone up and said I had a dropped call. It was dropped; I dropped it on purpose when I hung up. I was not getting back in with that niggas games. I had messed up and I refused to go a second round with trash. I wished that Nate and I could reconnect but I was going to have to be patient. He said he forgave me and I

could only pray that he had because tomorrow was the day that he was going to be in the same room with the man that I had an affair with.

We found my mother than went back to the room to get some rest for Candace's big day. My mother went back to the casino and stayed up all night and stated she was sick and didn't go to the wedding. I could see the disappointment on Candace's face and I told her that the most important people her and Mike will be there. We got dressed and she was gorgeous. She looked so pretty, I tried hard not to cry. Jennifer was beautiful too. The whole wedding party was pretty. The men were handsome and Nate sang for Candace after he walked her down the aisle. Pot later made a comment to Candace that he should have listened to the words and maybe I wouldn't look so unhappy. He had his nerve even if he was right; he had no room to talk shit about my husband. We rode the elevator together and Nate pulled me out of the elevator quickly and Pot and his cousin snickered. I was pissed because Nate's monkey of insecurity was showing big time and I wished he would not give Pot the satisfaction. If it was me, I thought, I would have told him to take a good look at what he tried to take, but that was me.

When we got back to the room, my mother was just getting back from the casino. Candace was hurt and she just went in her room after looking at my mother with gall. She had every right but she remained respectful and held her tongue. I went in the room with Candace and told her not to let it spoil her day and we changed to go eat at the buffet. We had fun and we celebrated the marriage of my oldest child.

On the way back home, Nate didn't say much and all I thought about is that I had to take my mother back to Los Angeles and she didn't even go to the wedding which is why I brought her. That's family for ya!

It felt eerie back at the apartment. Nate was still quiet and I try to get him to talk to me but, he said he was fine. After two days of the silent treatment I began to fear for my life. He had to symptoms of murder/suicide. I didn't want to be in the Daily Press as a victim and as soon as Mike and his mother went to the airport, I was at Candace's apartment with my things telling her I was back and no was not an option. I told her that Nate scared the hell out of me with his silence and I thought he was thinking of killing me. The paranoid and guilt monkey had me fearing for my life. In my mind, I didn't blame him and I knew he was not capable of murder but I was not taking any chances.

Candace accepted me back and I became Mabel, the cook, housekeeper, and daycare provider. I was at her beck and call. Dinner was always ready when she came home until Sweetie Peetie went too far with the Little Lord Fauleroy bullshit. I had to put him in his place after he went after my children. I told my children that they were not allow out of the room when they were home to keep the conflict down. I didn't like chaos and this was their home not ours. Candace thought I was mad but I told her that I didn't want to ruin my welcome so I chose to stay out of their way. I told her that I remembered the last time I left and I didn't want them to resent us being there.

One day, I heard her neighbor talking in the living room about me. Mandy was asking Candace if I was mad and what was wrong with me. I decided to join the conversation and let them know I was alright. I tried to be sociable but I was not in tune with the conversation of internet dating and cyber-sex. I had enough of the flesh getting me in trouble and I was not going to allow myself to go there again. I got my best friend VSOP and started drinking shots. The children were bused to school so I didn't have to worry about driving drunk. After an hour a several shots, I started laughing at the feeble conversation of men and the drama. I then started to cry. I cried out that I didn't belong there and that I was in hell. I got up and stumbled to my room and continued to drink while I watched Snapped, a cable show about why women kill. I was watching the show to know the signs so I wouldn't kill someone.

The next week, I went to the apartment complex where I had put in an application. I spoke to the manager and told her I was desperate. I told her that my life was falling apart and I started crying. I told her about Katrina, my separation from my husband, and ruining the relationship with my daughter. She looked at my application and took me to see an apartment. She told me that I had the apartment but I needed the move in money. I told her that I had it. I went to the bank and withdrew a thousand dollars from my credit card and got a money order for the move-in fee. I praised God for the blessing and my new life. I vowed to stay in his will and not stray. I had learned my lesson. I went back to Candace house and got my things and Jennifer, Nate Alex and I moved that day. I told Candace that I appreciated her putting up with us and that I'm sorry for the outburst about being in hell. It was truly a mental hell, but I didn't belong there.

I needed my own space and God had blessed me with it.

I withdrew another thousand dollars to buy me a bedroom set and necessities like linen, cookware, and a dining room set from Kmart. The children and I were very grateful for our own place and we had a little celebration of our own. We thanked God. I called Pot to help get the children's furniture from Candace's garage and he came to help. He brought the furniture to the apartment and then took a grand tour. We had gotten to my bedroom, and he sat on my bed. My skin crawled and I asked him to get up. I told him that he didn't belong on my bed and that it was inappropriate. He obliged, but I could tell that he expected a little appreciation and thank you would have to suffice. I was still on Welfare and the apartment was affordable living. My rent was $409 a month for a 3 bedroom. God was showing me favor and I appreciated it. I wanted so much to please him. Nate came to get the children every weekend and I would go to Sandra house and spend the night and go to church from Colton.

My children would often look tired and smell like fish grease. I would try to talk to Nate and he would say that they were fine. I could see that they weren't fine and the smell was awful. I didn't want him to think that I was being mean so I went to his place unannounced and the apartment was a wreck. The carpet had stains and the kitchen was a mess. Nate was in his room playing the keyboards and my children were laying in a mess in the living room. They were adapting to living like cursed people and I had had it. I yelled at the children for accepting this and they should be helping their daddy, not living like bums. I started to clean the apartment when Nate told me to stop and that he was going to get it. I asked him what was that smell as I look around as is I was looking for a dead animal. I told Jennifer and Nate Alex to get their things and told Nate that they won't be back. I refused to let them live like that. I told him that he could come and see them whenever he wanted, but they didn't deserve to be treated bad for our mistakes. Jennifer and Nate Alex were sad for their dad, but they were ready to get out of there. I asked them why they never said anything and they stated that they felt sorry for their dad.

Every holiday, I would invite Nate to the dinners usually given at Candace's place and one night we were drinking. I was drinking Jose Cuervo, my drink of choice. We were playing my game of choice, Scrabble when I started talking about Nate so bad that all the feeling I had kept to myself had been release like a flood gate had given way. I don't remember a thing, but I was told that I told Nate that he wasn't a man and that I didn't need a nigga or a dick. I needed a man and it was obvious that he was not one. I was lashing out because of desperation. I wanted my husband back, but he did nothing to help the situation. He complained all the time and he looked like crap. His clothes smelled and were dingy. His once kissable lips were chapped and peeling and he needed a shave. All this was said in an alcoholic tone. I finally passed out and fell face first. I awoke to a bruised face and the skin missing from my top lip. All I could do was thank God that I didn't lose any teeth.

I went to Candace and asked her to let daddy come and stay with her until things could work out between us. She agreed but instead of it going the way I thought, they became allies against me. Candace began to take care of Nate like I did and then complained that she did it. His family refused to give him anymore more money because they said he would have to use the money to come back to New Orleans. After six months, Candace was no longer able to provide for her daddy. Nate didn't want to go back home and leave his children and when he received the money changed his mind. He needed the money so he used it to rent a room in Moreno Valley so he could be closer to his job.

I was now in my place for three months and things were getting away from me. I had no money to make the car payment because the Welfare went to our living expenses. Melanie and Kevin didn't pay me back the money that I had loaned them. I became a bill collector and not their sister. I finally realized that I was not getting the money back and told them that they didn't owe me anything. By this time, I needed help big time. I had an urgency to put money on my boost mobile account and so I spent my last to get the minutes. I put the minutes on my phone while I was at Sandra's apartment waiting for her to come back from her doctor's appointment and within an hour my phone rang. It was the County of San Bernardino offering me a job for the position of an Employment Service Specialist. I was just praying that the Lord show me what I was supposed to be learning to get out of this pit I was in. I accepted the position and wrote down the information for orientation. I thanked the Human Resource Officer and hung up the phone. I began telling the Lord everything that I learned of to not let my anger cause me to sin, to love myself like Jesus loved me, to treat people with respect and to always stand up for what was right and to always follow the rules. I was thanking and praising him for his goodness and mercy. I thanked him for provisions and being on time. When Sandra came back, I told her about the minutes and the urgency to put them on the phone and she looked at me like I was crazy. I had a job and it was given to me by God. Thank you, Jesus.

I couldn't wait to get home to tell the children that God gave mom a job. I was going to be doing something that I love to do which is to help people. I knew a lot about Human Services and I was excited about this new challenge. I knew I didn't want to be an Eligibility Worker, but I had been to Job Club three times. I was ready to be employed. I didn't even know how much I was going to be paid but I was happy to be working. I was two months behind in my car payment and the loan company was threatening to repossess my car and then I would not have transportation to get to the training in San Bernardino. I had no one to call for help and I sat there fearing that my car could be taken in the middle of the night. I told them that I had a job but I would not be starting it until October which was two months away.

The loan officer stated that they could not

wait that long. I was advised to get the money somehow and I would qualify for a deferment for three months and the car payment would be due by the time I got my first paycheck. I told them to give me a little time and I will call them back. I called my Pastor at the Baptist church in Riverside CA. and told him what was going on. He told me that he had to talk to the Deacons and someone will be in touch.

Within an hour a decision was made and the Finance Officer from the church called me for the information. God had sent me another angel and I was again thankful. I saw him working on my behalf and I was truly grateful. Thank you, Jesus.

In the mist of all my blessings, Nate was constantly being cursed.

Chapter 36

After six months, Nate had moved down the hill because Candace's husband felt that Nate was taking advantage of Candace because she would always complain about money and that she didn't have enough. Nate had not gotten a job and her husband felt that if Nate was not there, things would get easier and he was coming home soon and didn't want to be taking care of another man. Nate was offended and left and moved to his friend's house for two weeks when his friends wife said that he had to go. Nate received money from his family to move back to New Orleans, but Nate used the money to rent a room in Moreno Valley and soon found a Job. I was happy for him and felt that maybe he could get his life and confidence back. I allowed enough time for him to get settled before I started asking the children if they had spoken to their father. The answer was always no. I called Nate and asked why he was not calling the children and he gave me some lame excuse and I would tell him not to forget why he didn't go back to New Orleans. Being agreeable as always, he continued to be missing in action until one day I received a call from him. I thought he was calling for the children, but found that he was calling because he had gotten in an accident where he was at fault and his car was totaled in the collision. All this for trying to pick up a dollar he had dropped on the floorboard of the car.

It had been months since he moved and only saw his children on Sunday at church service. He never called and then when he gets in trouble he calls not to speak to his children but to whine to me.

Some men just don't get it. I sat there with the phone speechless while he did all the talking about being stupid and I could imagine the monkey on his back growing like a gorilla on the Empire state building. I just listened and refused to stop him which is what he wanted me to do. I then told him I had nothing to say and hung up. I was a single mother of two children and I was not looking for one more. He never once came to Victorville to see the children when he had the car so what did it matter to me. My only thought was now he had a legitimate reason for not seeing the children.

Transportation needed!

I wanted to leave the church that we both fellowshipped at but God told me that I had to say. I was stared at and treated disrespectfully but I was not going to be disobedient. Every Sunday, I went and the sermons were good, but the treatment was often unbearable. Sometimes Nate was looking like he was not taking care of himself and that made me feel bad. I noticed that I was conceiving a monkey of guilt. I was feeling bad that life was going well for me and the children and my family would say things like I was wrong for bringing him back to California only to dump him.

This only made the monkey grow: in size and strength. I would drink to feel better and often drank until I fell asleep. Rumors service that I was now an alcoholic and that my life was falling apart. I became a drunken service of the Lord and I felt I was losing control. I prayed for deliverance and the pain to stop. I didn't want to be a single parent.

Even God knew that Adam needed a companion and so did I. I had done the single parent crap with Candace and now I had two children. I resented Nate for putting me in this position and then I started to resent myself as I consumed more VSOP. I continued to watch Snapped so that I wouldn't do anything foolish, but my situation was completely different. Nate didn't have any money and the property in New Orleans was signed over to Netty. I thought about Social Security and then just laughed at the negative thoughts while rebuking the devil for planting the seeds of murder.

I wasn't going to be the next reality show on television and I did want to go to Heaven. I wasn't sinless, but I was a Child of God and knew that a life was not mine to take. I continued to involve Nate in the children's life. I told him of their progress and when they were sick. I often heard from him that he wished he could do something but I knew he wouldn't even if he could. His monkeys were too many and prevented him from being there for his children or me. I would often respond that I knew that he would like to help but I wasn't calling for that and if it was me, I would like to know what was going on with my children.

Nate was a good guy. He just had been accustomed to leaving everything up to me to solve and I did what every good wife did. I made him look good. I took care of everything and I guess that was why I didn't miss him. It did however take me a good eighteen months for me to realize that life was less stressful.

Problems were solved quicker because I didn't have to consult Nate before taking any action and I was the only one to handle it, so there was no decision to make or to see if he would take charge and handle a problem.

I soon realized that I had been led astray, hoodwinked and bamboozled. I had been looking for my daddy and my daddy had been dead since I was eight years old. The pain became less and less until it was completely gone. I could see Nate and not feel resentment.

Jennifer and Nate Alex were happy to have a place of their own. The made new friends and also found that some old friends already lived in the complex. They were allowed to go outside, but were not permitted to enter into anyone's apartment. Jennifer didn't agree with my decision, but she was only thirteen and I had the final say so. I had rules and they were not up for negotiation. I took my job as parent and overseer of my children seriously. God had given me authority over them and I was not going to disappoint him.

Nate Alex was eleven at the time and was very much a child and he was often ridiculed for his way of thinking. More of the same treatment from kids at his father's apartment. Kids would bully him and called him awful names. He endured being called gay as if a child of eleven had a sexual orientation. He was a child. He did not use profanity, and he did not disrespect adults. He was helpful and would volunteer his help at the office and the club house in the complex. He would ride his scooter and bike when it was allowed.

I taught him to follow the rules and to have respect for authority. He would tell the manager when kids were destroying the property, like them trying to knock down the gate, playing in the laundry room, or when the kids tried to take rides on the front gate as cars came through. He would complain to me about the activity that went on at the playground: the rude behavior, the fights, and the threats of physical harm. Nate Alex would talk of marijuana being smoked in front of children like it was normal. He stopped going to the playground and often stated that he hated the apartment because the people were ghetto.

Kids would throw raw eggs at their bedroom windows and because we lived on the second floor, the stains stayed there until we left even though I notified the management of the incident. One day, while outside playing with a six year old he thought was a friend. Nate Alex got hit in the head with a rock. He had blood streaming down his face and I ran to get him. I was sitting on the patio watching him playing with marbles in the dirt when he screamed and got up holding his head. When I saw the blood, I sprung into to action. I ran out the door and Jennifer followed. The little boy said he was playing and I asked him if this looked like play. I told him to go get his mother and he looked at me like I was crazy. Jennifer knew where he lived and said she will go get his mother. I took Nate Alex upstairs to take care of the wound that was centimeters from his eye. I was comforting him when in walks a woman dressed for Halloween and it was in the summer. She had neon blue streaks in her hair, facial piercing and tattoos all over in arms. I took one look and knew why this had happened. I told her that she should keep a better eye on her son and teach him the importance of not throwing rocks. She was very apologetic and she made her son also apologize.

Nate Alex was also locked in the trash bin area and taunted by kids in the complex. He went to take the trash out which was one of his chores and when he didn't return, Jennifer went looking for him. She found the kids calling Nate Alex gay and threatening to beat him up and with language that children shouldn't even be hearing let alone be using. Jennifer called me at work to tell me she had to shoo them away like vultures after dead meat. Nate Alex was traumatized often until I told him that it would be best that he stay in the house unless he had a buddy system of protection. I would take them outside to fly kites or take them to the pool, but other than that they became prisoners in their own home.

Jennifer, on the other hand tried to fit in. She would follow the ring leader of the apartment gang. She later told me it was for protection at school. At the pool while they swam, men would drink beer while watching the little girls swim like they were watching a movie. I went to the pool to watch over them for safety purposes. I would position my chair to watch them watch the girls. I once had to tell a man to stop looking at my daughter like she was lunch and he apologized but that didn't stop him from looking at other girls the same way he once looked at Jennifer. Her friends would often ask her why I was tripping and Jennifer would get embarrassed. I saw Jennifer changing and I tried to talk to her and she would tell me that she was following the rules and I left it at that.

One of the rules were that my children be at home when I got home from work. I always wanted to know where they were in case something happened I would know where to go to get them. On this occasion, Jennifer was not home and I went looking for her. She was near sighted and didn't see me from across the courtyard. I was praying that that child didn't break the rule about going into anyone's apartment, but she did.

I started walking across the courtyard like Sophia on the color purple. I was angry and wondering. How long had this been going on? There were rumors that the gang leader lived with a known pedophile. I checked and he was on the Meagan Law website. I got to the door and knocked. When the door opened, Jennifer looked like a deer in headlights. She knew she was busted. I didn't have to say anything. She just walked out of the apartment and down the stairs. I was angry, so I didn't say anything right away. I was still walking like Sophia and she was trailing behind me and I told her to catch up. She continued to take her own sweet time like I had did something wrong. I turned around and in the calmest voice told her that she knew she was wrong. She acted like nothing was wrong. She was carrying a cupcake and I knocked it out of her hand but it took all the strength in my being not to knock her on her tail. I told her she had better keep up and I turned and headed toward our apartment.

We got to the apartment and I sat down and she followed. I began to tell her of the dangers of going into other's apartment and that I was uncomfortable because I didn't know the occupants and for my peace of mind, I needed to be able to trust her with my rules. She began to roll her eyes stating that she didn't know what the big deal was and that I was too controlling. Her attitude shocked me and I stopped talking. I told her to go in her room and I went to mine. I returned with a wide leather belt called bad belt. I took the buckle off just in case it slipped out of my hand. I wouldn't want to hit my child with the metal. When I opened her door, I saw the deer eyes again and I began to finish the conversation and the only thing that spoke was bad belt and he spoke volumes. By the time the conversation was over, Jennifer was on the floor and I asked her if there was any confusion about the message and she whimpered and stated no. I left her to nurse her wound ego.

About an hour had pass, when Jennifer enter my room carrying a note that she handed to me and exited just as quick as she came.

6/24

Dear Mom,

I am so sorry for the way I acted today. It was very irresponsible and uncaring. I do care for you more than anything. I just wasn't thinking. I just wanted to have a little fun. I am so sorry. I am not grown but I am growing so I guess I wanted to know how it feels to do what you want to do and that got me in trouble. I am sorry for being disobedient. I don't want to be a burden to you. I am sorry causing you grief. I want to be a good daughter. I am so sorry. I hope you accept my apology. I love you more than anything.

Love,

Jen

I thought even through the hard task of spanking my daughter, she understood and felt that I was right to do what I had to do. Jennifer was a good child and I attended to keep her that way. I was determined not to let our life circumstance corrupt my child.

There was one girl that kept talking about Jennifer so bad and Jennifer feeling that she had something to prove went to the laundry room to fight. When I got home from work, She was in the bathroom breathing hard as she began to tell me what happen. She showed me where the girl snatched to of her braids out from the roots leaving a rectangular bald spot on the side of her head. When I found out that she went to the fight, I became angry. I told her never to go to a fight and not to throw the first punch. Fighting was always a last resort to self-defense. I told Jennifer that I was disappointed in her decision then I told her to always secure her braids in the event of a fight by tying them into a knot of tucking them into you shirt, taking off all jewelry and apply Vaseline.

What can I say? I am from L.A Westside. I may have moved out of the ghetto, but the ghetto lives inside me for protection. The threats of bullying got so bad that I had to bring out the ghetto in me. My children were scared to go outside. They told me of lies that were told on them by the girl that Jennifer had previously fought. The rumors caused Jennifer to be threatened by the leader on the complex posse. That girl was as big as me and looked like she could be Jennifer's mother. I went to the girl's apartment that had lied on Jennifer and I addressed the mother and five kids with four baby daddies and one in the oven. I told her that I was through playing with her and treating her like she had an ounce of intelligence. I told her that I raised my children different but not to get it twisted and that I was from the hood just like she was and that I had been around the block and was not afraid to go again. That stopped the harassment and I knew my children were grateful. They were not with me when I approached the lady, so I was still mom to them.

Chapter 37

I started thanking him for the day, the air, and the itch I satisfied with a scratch. I saw everything with new eyes. I saw God working on my behalf and I knew I was in his favor. I went to Wal-Mart and I saw the same man that I had passed up at the Apple Valley a year ago selling his CD's at the Victorville store. I decided to bless as I had been blessed and found that I was the one blessed again. I only had eight dollars on me and that same man I thought of as a peddler I now saw a man working for a living. Maybe it was because he name dropped my Pastor and First lady but I gave him the money and he gave me the CD for $2.00 less because that was all I had on me. As I walked to my car I began to rip the plastic off the cover because I wanted to hear what he was about and when I hear the first track I was amazed. That man was gifted and I drove over to him with my window down and told him that he was anointed and had a great gift. I thanked him for me and told him not to leave because I was going to get more money to buy the other CD. I came back and bought the other CD. I listened to the CD every time I was in the car and at work. I refused to let people make copies so he wouldn't be bootlegged.

His message made me yearn for the word and I began to live better. I made it a point to outdo myself the next day and each day I was better that the day before. I started to learn intimacy and relationship and stopped being ruled by my flesh. One day I went to Food 4 Less, a grocery store, and saw the liquor and it made my stomach quiver. I no longer wanted a drink and soon didn't even like the taste of wine. I was delivered yet again this time from alcohol. I say this because I had a problem with alcohol and I thought I may have been becoming an alcoholic. I was able to see the monkeys that were causing me so much pain and damage to my life. I was able to deny my flesh and soon I didn't feel lonely. I was okay by myself and felt that when it was time to date I would do just that date.

I was at peace and it no longer hurt to see Nate. I still loved him but I felt that I couldn't live with him and I was fine with that. I even knew the right words to say to my customers at work and I truly loved my Job. God began to give me favor at my complex. Even though I had a job and my lease had ended my rent remained low. I even went to them to see if they made a mistake and was told it was correct.

One day I saw a house and I never go to open houses but on this Sunday after church the children and I went to see a house around the corner from the apartments. When I walk through the door I felt this vibe that was peaceful. It had the same flow as the Louisiana home but bigger. Before I could see the whole house the Lord told me *not now, next year*. Jennifer and Nate Alex had already picked their rooms and didn't understand why I told them it was time to go. When I got to the car, I told them that the Lord said *not now, next year*. Nate Alex asked me what if someone moved into it and I told him that they will move back out.

I believed what I had heard and this time I had the word of God on my side not just the desire to have something nice. I knew that I was a child of God the most high and I was faithful. I got along well with others at work and even people that I didn't know would strike up a conversation with me. I smiled all the time because I wanted to make some ones day and because I knew that another day was given to me and I intended to make the best out of it.

Sandra called me to ask if she could come and stay with me for a while because her son was moving and she had no income to provide not even her basic need. I felt that God had blessed me and I wanted to bless someone else and here was my chance. I moved her in and paid for her furniture to be moved

to Victorville. She was my sister/friend and she was in need. I bought her basic needs and some of her wants. I wanted her to know that I had her back. She moved into the apartment and we got along fine.

She had been injured on her job and was suing the company. I was not looking for anything in return because I knew that that was not my blessing. I would encourage her and give her compliments about her strength and pray for weaknesses. She on the other hand would speak about every imperfection that I had. I would just look at her and tell her she had jokes. Then I would say that the sooner or later she would see that I had a lot of confidence in myself and I was made perfect in God's eye. I told her that she needs to see what God saw in her and maybe she would not have to try to put me down.

She would say that people thought I had motives for taking her in other than to help a friend. I assured her that I had no motive and that I just saw a need and I was being obedient. She started to go to church with us but the lust monkey was on the woman and she had her eye on the neighbor across the patio. I would work all day and she did nothing but I did think she would cook from time to time. Instead, I had another mouth to feed and we had discussed her role living with us. One day, when I came home she began telling me about the neighbors comings and goings and I told her I was not interested. I went to the kitchen and decided to make chicken salad. She came into the kitchen while I was chopping the seasonings and began yelling at me about messing up the kitchen. I would have cleaned it up but I wasn't finished and I asked her what was she doing besides spying on people. I told her that I could use a little help and she walked off.

I finished the chicken and she did clean the kitchen and then went outside. I went to my room with my fresh chicken salad sandwich and watched TV in my room to give her some space.

The next day she gave me the silent treatment and I started to think back on what I had said and I found nothing that warranted that kind of behavior.

I suggested that if she came into the kitchen to help instead of spying on people the kitchen wouldn't look so bad. I didn't flip out when she said I had no knees and that my breast hung too low and why was she looking at me like that anyway.

Jennifer was sitting in the living room and she told me that she heard Sandra on the phone making plans to leave. I couldn't believe that she was taking it this far. I went to talk to her and she was angry. Again, I scanned my memory to see what I could have said that would cause this reaction. She told me that she didn't want to talk and I told her that we needed to talk about what made her so angry and she started to yell at me. I told her that I didn't know what was wrong but she will respect me and we will need to talk this through because we I couldn't live with dissention in my home. She went past me and went into my son's room and unplugged the lamp that she had given him.

I watched as she went into the bathroom and got all of her personal items. I called her name and asked why she was so mad. She began to talk about how I treated Jennifer and that she was supposed to be my friend. What did Jennifer have to do with this? She begin saying that I talk to Jennifer like she was grown and that Jennifer is just a child. I told her that Jennifer was being exposed to all kind of foolishness at school and it was my job as a parent to make life make sense. I told her that I didn't want to see Jennifer on the internet showing all her shit to get attention like someone's daughter I know.

Sandra's daughter had put exotic pictures on the internet of herself dressed in a swimsuit that looked like a bandage. She had tattoos all over her body and I felt sorry for her. I always said that monkeys raise monkeys. It was obvious that the girl was looking for love in the wrong place. Her actions were screaming for attention and her dumb ass mother was too busy thinking of herself and left her daughter to the wolves.

Sandra was also an internet dater and she once told me that that is why I didn't have friends. Mind you, she needed me because those so called friends couldn't take her in when she lost her job and her apartment and her 350Z. She didn't have a pot to piss in or a window to throw it out. I was there for her. I bought all her necessities and cigarettes were not cheap and I gave her a comfortable place to stay. My children were respectful and they did not complain that I spent a lot of time trying to encourage her. In my line of work, I dealt with people like that every day. I knew it was fear and I was trying to give her time to see where she was in life and to let her know that I was there as a sister friend to support her while she got on her feet.

When she called to tell me that she needed a place to stay, I told her that it would be perfect because the children was getting out of school for the summer and I was worried about them being idled. I think minors need supervision even though state law states that child thirteen and over don't need a sitter. I guess that's why we had so many babies having babies. I trusted Jennifer, but I was not that naïve to think that she was immune to hormones. Nate Alex was still being harassed at the apartment complex, but I couldn't make them stay in the apartment for the entire summer. It was a win-win situation because the alternative was to ask Nate to come back home and that was out of the question.

She had it twisted when she started telling me that she was under the impression that she just had to watch the children. I replied, telling her that she still had to take care of herself and that included eating. I bought the food and since she was not working she could have had dinner ready or even started. Hell, she couldn't even take meat out of the freezer to be defrosted and I was not big on eating out. I prided myself on cooking a home-cooked meal for my children. Instead of watching my children, Sandra was watching my son's friend father come and go. She was either having cyber-sex or sitting on the patio that faced Nate Alex's friend apartment and would get giddy when the man came out for a smoke.

One day, Jennifer came to me and asked me if Sandra had graduated from high school and I thought she did. Jennifer went on to tell me that she had to read her MySpace page because she didn't understand some of the words. I was concerned because Jennifer was not old enough to have a page herself. When Sandra and I were alone, I told her that I didn't want Jennifer looking at her MySpace and if she needed help, I would help her. She agreed and I thought that was that. Sandra was the only one that I had as a friend and adult that I talked to. I had no relationship with my sisters and the women at my church were cliquish and back biting. Candace was out in left field somewhere acting like she didn't have any home training and so I kept our visits at a limit. Now Sandra was going off and I wondered what was wrong with women these days.

As Sandra was going around the apartment packing her belongings, she passed Jennifer and started to yell at her. Jennifer was shocked and wondered what was wrong with her. Sandra had assumed that I had discussed what happened last night but that only proved that she didn't have a clue about me. I didn't put my children in grown people's business. I only explained what was going on after they had been exposed. I jumped between Jennifer and Sandra and told her she better step off. Sandra knew I was no longer in an encouraging mood. You don't fuck with my children. It was not tolerated at all. I was like a lioness protecting her cub and I would fuck you up over my children. I told Jennifer to go to her room until this was over. Jennifer did what she was told without saying a word. Sandra told me that I treated Jennifer like a grown up and it seemed like she was my best friend instead of her. I told her that Jennifer was my child and she trumped even best friends. She walked pass me and went outside and sat on the stairs. I left her alone and figured she was grown and I was not going to coddle her behavior. I went into the living room and was watching television when she stormed but in the apartment with Jefferson, her son.

He was a handsome man with a six pack, golden skin and strong facial features. He had education and a good job working in Finance. I greeted him and invited him in as Sandra grabbed some of her things and went to put them in the car. Jefferson turned to me and asked what had happened. I was clueless myself. I told him about the chicken and kitchen incident and then what was happening, this uncalled display of ungratefulness. I was not going to play into the tantrum that she was acting on. She came back into the apartment and took her plants that looked nice in my apartment. I was sorry to see her go, but I was also shocked at her behavior.

Days had pass since Sandra had left and God started to deal with me about what had happened. I was not to take it personally because I did nothing wrong. Sandra was dealing with more issues that I was not aware of and if she didn't want to talk about the incident, I was going to leave it alone as well.

Candace called a week later and told that Sandra had asked her if she could come and stay with her. I felt sorry for her and realized that God had prepared me to soften my heart. I told Candace to take her in since none of her own children were willing to take her in for whatever reason. Candace explained that the reason she was asking is because of the other woman that she had showed charity too, but this was a different matter altogether. The other woman had taken my checks and went on a shopping spree courtesy of me. She completely shut down my bank activity and I had to send a police report to the District Attorney's office for bad check writing. I explained to Candace that she was being used and that the girl had a man while Candace was taking care of her two children alone while Gouda's daddy was in New Orleans finishing his apprentice program for electrical engineer.

Sandra would talk about me to Candace and because Candace had her own issues with me it seemed like a perfect fit in a sick world. Day after day, Candace heard from Sandra how I was over the top and that I treated Jennifer like a grown up. That only added to Candace's monkeys already on her back.

A year had passed since I had gone to an open house and saw this beautiful, four bedroom home. During the walk through, God told me *not know, next year*. My faith was strong and I knew that the house was mine, I just had to be patient. I went to the apartment and put the 8X10 photo of the house on my dresser in my bed room and every morning I would chant *next year, Lord* and then go to work. I told my coworkers about the house and told them that next year I would be in it. The excitement was there but, I think they thought I just had wishful thinking.

Candace in the meantime had rented a three bedroom house and her and Nate moved in. I was happy for her, but I was not happy with the neighborhood. I tried to talk her out of moving there, but she thought I was jealous that she was getting a house. I didn't say another word. At least Nate was going to be living with her and I had a sense of security for her.

I moved into the house, that God told me in a year, on May 26, 2009. I originally went to put the blinds up and Candace had gotten Sandra and me to talk about our differences. She had installed all of them and I wanted to help her and she needed my help. She ended up moving in and we became sisters living together again. While working on the yard, I met a guy who knew how to hook up my dishwasher. I was thankful that God had sent me someone to provide that need. Sandra was taken by him and at the time I didn't think I had anything to worry about. She would say things that indicated that something was going on but she was grown. I did try to convince her of relationship and not just sex however a renewing of the mind is a personal choice.

Soon my handyman was a ghost and I asked Sandra about his whereabouts and she would just shrug her shoulders. I didn't want to pry or make her feel embarrassed so I stopped asking. I figured that she must have given up the diamond and it was finished. She became angry and quiet and I figured that she would talk when she was ready.

Sandra soon started to complain about not having the money to pay for her storage. I told her that she could move her furniture into my garage and she agreed. I paid for a truck and was given a huge discount on the mileage. That was God favor because I was blessing someone as he blessed me. Sandra's mom came and spent the weekend and I didn't mind.

She was disabled and walked with a walker and I catered to her like a daughter. Sandra would tell Jennifer that her mother was going to milk it for all she could. I didn't understand why she would say such a thing about her mother. My mother was not my wish list mother but I loved, honored and respected my mother. I even asked my mother to come to live with me, but even she knew that was not a good idea. Not that I wouldn't take care of her but she had painful memories and wanted to keep them buried while I dealt with my monkeys.

One Sunday, I invited Sandra's mother to come to church with us and she agreed. She seem happy to be able to worship and on the way back to her son's home where she lived, she talked about her treatment from her grandchildren. I felt sorry for her and I had been talking to Sandra about letting her mother come to say so she could have some peace while dealing with her disabilities.

Sandra would always say she would talk to her mother, but a decision was never made so I thought she said no. While on the way home from church Sandra's mom began complaining again and I asked Sandra if it was okay to ask her mom what we had discussed. Sandra said it was all right so I brought up the subject of her moving with us. She like the idea and it was like that was the first that she ever heard of the idea.

Later that evening, I spoke to Sandra about

her mother's reaction and that if she was not sure about her mother living with us she should tell me what was going on and Sandra assured me that she didn't mind. I blessed her with transportation to bring yet another apartment full of furniture to my garage and thought they would eventually move together. Sandra was very secretive and I wasn't thinking about her business but she was antsy. I didn't need anything from Sandra and she didn't have to hide her business but I felt that was just her way so I said nothing.

The truth came out when my oven malfunctioned and she left my children fifteen minutes before I got off from work to go out to dinner with her family that came to visit her new home. Her cousin had dripped oil on my clean driveway and when I got home I noticed the dirt on the driveway but I didn't think anything of it at the time. As I came into the house, my children met me at the door and told me that she and her mother went to a buffet restaurant and I walked into the kitchen and saw raw chicken on the counter. I couldn't understand how she could have done this. Sandra fried the best chicken and I even praised her chicken to the only church member that I could talk too. I was tired and now I had thawed chicken that had to be cooked. I told the children that we were going to grill it and they were thrilled.

They helped me get everything together and I was outside watching the chicken and thinking how a person that I helped so much could do this? As I was finishing the chicken Sandra and her family came back to the house and proceeded to watch a movie while her cousin spoke of how full he was. I told my children to set the table so that they would stop talking to that idiot. We talked at dinner about their day and I could hear Sandra sucking her teeth as if to tell us we were too loud as we ate dinner. I paid her no attention and continued to eat and talk to my children.

I had an appointment at 7:00 to get some money back from a man for a car deal gone badly and I wanted Sandra to go with me but that was out of the question. It was obvious that she was a taker and incapable of being a giver, so I told my children what I had to do. I told them to get their bats in case something went wrong. I didn't think I was in danger but I didn't know this man to well and I was going to his home and I didn't want to go alone. As we left, I noticed that the car in my driveway was leaking oil. I came back into the house and asked her cousin to move his car outside the gate onto the dirt so my driveway would not get stained up. Sandra was furious but I wouldn't find out until the next day. I came home and asked to speak to Sandra and her mother. I asked what their intentions and plans for the future were. They both looked at me like I said something in another language. I told Sandra that I was still waiting for an answer to my proposal to pay for her GED classes. She got upset and started yelling at me and I was trying to keep my cool. I explained that I was concerned about her behavior and her total disregard for my children with leaving them without anything to eat and then there was the fan incident where she yelled at my children for using her mother's dusty fan that was not being used and was stored in the garage.

Chapter 38

I realized that Sandra and her mother was using the central air while we were in school and work but would cut it off when we came home. One day, Nate Alex was dripping sweat from his forehead and Jennifer being told by Sandra that she could not turn on the air ran and got the fan that she had seen in the garage. Sandra started screaming at Jennifer because she didn't ask her mother if she could use her fan. Jennifer explained that her mother was taking a nap and because she wasn't using it she didn't think she would mind. Sandra was still yelling. I told her to lower her voice and stop talking to my child that way. I told her I didn't see the big deal. Her mother was not using the fan and it was apparent that Nate Alex needed to be cooled off. Sandra told me that was not the point.. I told her that my children didn't mind that they were living in their home and that I was spending a lot of their quality time to mend her wounded spirit. They knew that Sandra was broke and not once did they complain that I was spending money to take care of her needs and she was yelling at them about a fan.

I told her that she was selfish and that she needed to quit. She said she needed to go because she said that I embarrassed her by telling her cousin to move the car and this was her house too and more rumors surfaced. This time it was my sexual orientation. My mother called me to tell me she had a dream that Sandra and I got married and that hurt me to my core. I told my mother that she should know me and that was not me.

I knew that Jake ran the rumor mill and that he had put that crap in my mother's head. I still was hurt because she had to entertain the garbage to have a dream like that. I told my mother that I had to go and hung up the phone to cry from the hurt that my mother didn't know that I knew that word of God. I was an Eve and I needed an Adam, not an Ava.

Days later, my mother called me back and gave me Psalms 69. I didn't have my bible readily available and I asked her to read the chapter. She told me it was too long and it would take too much time and I told her to hang up then. I was through with the innuendos and the jokes about me and my need to be obedient. I was determined to keep the monkeys off my back and I was not going to let even my mother attempt to put them on my back. She interrupted me while I was saying that I was tired of all the mean things that were said about me.

She started to read the 69 chapter of Psalms and I listened. When she finished, I was in tears and this time it was relief because I knew that she understood what I was going through and because the words gave me comfort. Confirmation at last. I knew what was happening. All the mean attitudes toward me were an attempt to knock me down and to discourage me from my spiritual walk to the intimacy with God. My relationship was getting stronger and all the difficulties I was facing were an ill-fated attempt to distract me from my destiny. I had a word and something to say, but what?

Chapter 39

I went to work the next day with a newfound strength. I was not going to let my supervisor or my coworkers get to me. I was a true witness and my light was shining. My birds were protected and I had a confidence, not in myself but in God. He was my protector and I was no longer afraid. So what my supervisor said I was bipolar.

I didn't care about the whispers behind my back. I wore my heels and my clothes well and my hair even though I had to paid for it was great. I thanked God for everything in my life, even my haters. A coworker from another unit said I would make a certain Katt proud for all the haters I had.

I handled my caseload and took care of my customers like I was lead to do. I never mention religion but my customers would often asked what church I attended and I would ask them what made them think I went to church and they would reply that it was something about the way I was.

I was pleased to be a good witness and I would tell them that I worshipped in Riverside. Often they would get disappointed because the church was far and they had transportation issues. I told them it was not the church, but relationship that was important.

I continued to get called into the office for complaints by customers who didn't want to participate with the program, but never was I told of any customers who liked my approach. I always had respect and compassion for my customer and to help them decide how the program could best help them. I would then be criticized by my superiors that I took my job too serious. I would think that that was a compliment because we were talking about people's lives and families. I was told that I was not supposed to appraise and that was just a word that was used to label an activity.

The manager told me that the handbook was written by bureaucrats that didn't know what they were talking about and my reply was that until they came up with a way to get the handbook changed, I was going to continue using it. I guess he didn't like my answer because I was given a memo of concern for threats to a coworker, Insubordination and refusing a directive from a supervisor. They were treating me like a whistle blower and I had stumbled on to the illegal practices of padding numbers to make the program look successful while the customers suffered.

My coworkers would often joke about having job security and I didn't find it funny. The mission statement that I proudly hung in my cubicle was a farce and I think that is why my supervisor gave it to me, but I was honored to have it because I believed in it. I was asked by my manager if I cared so much because I was once a customer myself as the two men that had me in an office alone snickered at the question. I respectfully replied if it gave me empathy and compassion that was a good thing. I was livid at the interrogation and insulted by the total disrespect. I answered their questions as best that I could but nothing I had to say would be right. I was interrogated for an hour and fifteen minutes and that was because the office was closing and all employees had to be out of the building. I left the office feeling like I had gotten through to the men only to find out the next morning that my words didn't matter. I had not convinced the men that the program was being manipulated and it was not helping the customers but hindering them even more.

The Manager of the program called me into the office and we spoke for another hour while I tried to convince him that I meant well when he handed me a memo of concern that I had threaten a coworker, was insubordinate and that I refused a directive. In the memo, there were stereotypes of quotes that a black, belligerent person would say. They made me sound angry and hostile.

As I read the memo, I let my objections be known and the manager agreed to change the tone and omit some of the quotes that were in the body of the letter. I got so tired of the corrections that I gave up. I told him that it was apparent that his mind was made up and that I didn't understand why he was doing this but it wouldn't work. I went back to my cubicle feeling like I was forced to sign the memo and I knew I would have to be extra careful in my tone and delivery of everything I said.

The coworkers in my unit were standoffish and mean. There was no longer eye contact and when I spoke to them, they shunned me by giving me one word answers while pretending to be too busy to talk to me. I received a lot of e-mails that were not important but had to be addressed so that I would not appear to be ignoring my superiors. This and other distractions were being used as a barrier to make me appear incompetent. I was overworked and underappreciated by my supervisor even though I had high employments and more people were earning their GED. I realized that I could not satisfy my superiors and now my coworkers had turned against me. I had no support from my unit and they would sabotage my work load to make it impossible for me to keep up and all the time I had wondered what I could had done to get the treatment from the ones I once thought of as friends.

The pain in my body was too hard to ignore. I was now taking Vicodin at work to mask the pain. I had a doctor's appointment and my doctor wanted to take me off work but I refused because I had too many bills and not enough time off work and I had not signed up for Aflac insurance to supplement any time off that I would need. I scheduled an appointment to sign up for the insurance but my body couldn't wait.

I had spoken to a coworker from another unit who told me that the job was not worth my health and that if I needed to leave I needed to draw on that faith that she knew I had and let God provide. I knew what she was saying but I also knew that I didn't want my unit to think that they broke me. I went back to my cubicle and all I could think about was trying to figure out what I had said or done to deserve such treatment.

The more I thought about it the more my body started to convulse. The pain was unbearable and I immediately called my doctor to tell her what was going on with my body and I was instructed to leave. I tried to call my supervisor but the call went to voicemail. I tried to e-mail her and I was not able to do that. I got up and went to the nearest supervisor in the office and told them that I was not feeling well and I was unable to find my supervisor and I was given permission to left.

As I was exiting my work area, I ran into my supervisor and by this time I could barely talk. I was starting to get scared because I had no idea of what was happening. My supervisor looked concerned and told me to leave and I did. When I got home, my husband helped me to the bed and I phoned my doctor who told me she would write an off work order and have it waiting for my husband to pick up.

My husband attempted to take the off work order to my office and was treated as so many customers were treated without regard of wellbeing and given no directions even though he told several people working there that he needed to see my supervisor as he identified who he was. After getting no help, he called me on the in house phone in the office and I told him to come home so I could make a copy of the order and that I will call my supervisor for her to know that he would be returning to give her information.

I called my supervisor and told her that my husband was in the office to give her the information and that he too received the run around. She told me that Nate could stand in the customer line and give it to the receptionist and we both knew what that meant. At times the line was out the door and she wanted my husband to wait in that line to give employee, not customer information. This was not what that line was for. I was her employee, not a customer, but yet again she continued to put me in my place. My tone made her change her mind and she told me to instruct my husband to come to the second floor and let the Wex working know that he was there. My husband received a warm welcome from the Wex worker who spoke highly of me. She was glad to get my supervisor for my husband. When the Wex had returned alone, my husband figured that my supervisor must have been in the middle of something so he had a seat. After fifteen minutes had passed, my husband heard someone calling his name and he went to the open door with my supervisor standing in the middle of it. She had stepped aside to let a man passed who my husband described as acting peculiar.

He said that he felt as if the guy was watching him as he spoke to my supervisor while handing her the off work order. My supervisor asked my husband if I had anything to tell her and he replied no and then Nate asked if she had anything that she wanted to tell me and she said no. As the conversation was ending, the man walked back into the office passing Nate and my supervisor and then she disappeared behind the door.

When my husband returned home he told me that something was going on and that he felt like the man that came out of the office was like her security from him. I asked him to describe the man. He told me it was a younger, Hispanic or dark Caucasian nicely dressed with a boyish face. My husband had described my manager and I wondered why they felt as if she needed protection or did he just wanted to know what kind of a person I truly was by my choice of a husband. I told my husband that they must have been shock to see such a mild mannered man and that had them scratching their heads. I guessed I was prejudged because I was a black woman with a voice and they took it for hostility instead of justice for all no matter what.

My off work order was for a month and it was hard on me because I was an active person and I didn’t understand what was happening. Everything in my life was good. I was back with my husband who had agreed to come back even though I left him. He left his job and trusted me and that I was in the will of God. We had started to have intercourse since our flesh told us we were still married under God but that quickly came to a halt. The Holy Spirit came to me and asked why I was going to make the same mistake that I had made seventeen years ago. We were not married and even though we had convinced ourselves that we were married we weren't under the law of the land. I told my husband that we would have to sleep in separate rooms until we remarried because I was going to be in the will of God.

My husband was reluctant and felt a little insecure because he thought that maybe I was not attracted to him or that he did not satisfy me. Neither was true. I needed to be in God's will and fornication was not going to do that. I had been there and done that and it cause me many years of drought in the intimacy department. Even though our first union produced two beautiful children, the act that cause the children was uneventful and often forgetful. I knew we were compatible because when we fornicated the sex was off the chain but after wedding it was like I was being going to the bathroom on. I tried to pretend to fake it until I felt it but often I was just faking it. There was no feeling there.

Chapter 40

It was thirteen years of drought and I didn't want to pretend ever again so fornication was out of the question. My children also knew the difference and said that we weren't married yet but they still needed an explanation when Nate moved to the spare bedroom on the other side of the house. I asked God for forgiveness and he forgave me. The monkeys started to be more pronounced in Nate because he equated sex with love and I told him time and time again that it was not him but it was me being in God's will. We often argued and I questioned whether he felt that he had made a mistake in coming back.

I often fell to my knees constantly praying for grace and mercy because it was often like torture. My home of serenity was quickly turning into chaos and confusion. We would talk to the children separately. I was encouraging the children that everything was going to be all right and that I asked for their dad back because God told me to and that was enough for them.

Just as I told them that the house that we now lived in, God told me in a year. It was six long months until God revealed to me that I had to renew my mind and that it was not my husband. The revelation was painful but I endured that pain for God to deal with me. I had to forgive Pot and Nate for the manipulation that I allowed to cause me to commit adultery. The one thing that I said I would never do and I did it willing. I did it willing. It was not an accident. I had a choice and I chose death over life. I broke down when the revelation hit me and I could only ask Nate to forgive me. I told him that I was waiting for him to get it together and it was me all along. I was carrying resentment for breaking the number one rule and I did it to myself.

I remember telling my pastor that I had did it and gave him reasons and excuses of feeling abandon and unloved and I now realized that I didn't love myself. I liked myself superficially. I was the size I wanted to be and I wore my clothes well. My face had finally came to it true form without the fat that surrounded it. I felt that my inside feeling were finally being seen. I had confidence and I was friendly but I couldn't keep me husband happy.

The monkey was there hiding and I couldn't fight or remove something I didn't know existed. While on my knees asking God why he told me to take my husband back and waited for an answer. I didn't receive it at that moment but when it hit me I was like a shattered mirror looking at the life that I called Christian. I was full of it and God put me in my face. I cried uncontrollably and Nate didn't know what to do. I told him that I had to go through it and that God was preparing me by making me see myself. I was not in control God was and as I accepted that revelation he begin to heal me.

My life was mine to do as I pleased but I now knew that I owed all I have or will ever have to God. I gave him my life and I gave it freely. Instead of practicing religion, I sought the Lord's word and will for my life and the closer I got the more was revealed to me. Jennifer would tell me that God had me down for a reason and that I needed to figure it out and she was right. I started to see that the closer I got to God and his word the more opposition I was receiving from family, friends and my Job. I told my supervisor that she didn't put me in my position and she was not going to remove me. I was not trying to be disrespectful but she was threatening me into submission of her way of wrong thinking. I was often convicted and felt that I would be betraying the people that I served if I did the job the way I was told to do it. I would not be helping people to self-sufficiency, I would be exposing them to more barriers and hindering them more with the way that I was told to do things. "Make it look pretty" What did that imply?

Suppression of my journal entries began because I was told that it sounded like I was blaming the program. I wasn't blaming the program. I believed in the program I just saw a lot of crooked under dealing the were not in the best interest of my people. Not black people, not women, but every customer that I came into contact with as an employee of the County. I took my job seriously and an unengaged customer, I took as my failure and I had no trouble passing it to a more compatible Specialist as long as they got the help on the program. I never thought that being good at my job would cause me so much trouble. I would hear complaints in the break room about the cars that were in the parking lot. Who cared? I knew how much my car payment was and I only thought what they had to do to be able to drive the cars they drove? I heard some of the stories of woman being used by baby daddy to make ends meet, the ugly old man that the young girls would let sleep with them because they didn't know any other way out, the abuse, both physical and mental that kept them in line by weak men who couldn't keep a woman any other way.

Epilogue

I felt for these people who have been lied to by the media and the music videos of young daughters barely dressed and dollar bills flying through the air while the men were clothed in the latest named brand gear they considered cool.

It is so bad that bitch is a common name for our daughters, sisters, mothers and some brothers while dawg/dog is common for our sons, brothers, our fathers and some sisters. We all need to wake up or the chickens will surely come home to roost right in our homes. Our mothers our jealous of our daughter because daddy paid attention to his child while some daddy's paid too close attention to their daughters and made them their lovers and there are mothers out there that allowed it to keep the man and the daughter is looked at like the other woman.

Watch out now, I think I just touched on a gorilla. The eyes are blind and it is disturbing and we complain when someone bless their food at a school function. We have taken God and prayer out of our schools and replaced him with metal detectors that don't even work. Who told you to take it out of your home? Magazines that tell our daughters that they are not good enough are replacing proverbs and being a virtuous woman. Grandmas trying to drop it like it's hot and know good and well they need an Epsom salt soak later that night. Kicking a dog is more offensive then the rape of a child. They give more jail time for abusing a dog then there is for abusing a child. Being politically correct is killing this world. Nigga is ignorant, not black, Bitch has always been a female dog and now it is common name calling for friends and enemies alike. Television is the number one babysitting and cartoons are on all night. My children still try to talk me into to letting them stay up well into the night for cartoons.

The cartoons are having more adult theme where cow utters likes like breast, yes droopy but breast all the same. There is violence fed to our children through cable television while we pay for the very thing that is destroying our families, while they laugh all the way to the bank. Charles always said all money ain't good money over a good game of Dominoes. What have you taught your children lately? Is it more than what the television or a day at school taught them? I have to have dinner every night with my children so they could purge all the negative things that they heard while they were out and about. What encouraging words did you give any child? My heart grieves for the children and how they are treated. Do what you want to do is very damaging to a child and the famous I don't care. It may seem like harmless words but they de-value and produce low self-esteem in our youth. Girls going to school with purple hair piercing and tattoos; boys in skinny jeans with hair the color of salt water taffy and why is a person's sexuality common conversation? Back in the day, we never talked about sex and now it discussed over dinner It matters to me because I was homeless with a home or parentless with a parent but I know that the cycle has to change for things to get better.

Value must be instilled back into children and adults alike. PC has been the downfall of the world but stupid is still stupid as a promiscuous person is still a Ho but still media gives us messages that it is just being free. Value of like and love.

Value of respect of our elders and parents and ourselves. Value of commitment when the media shows that's it okay to be pregnant out of wedlock and that a father is not needed. I valued the time when my father took me to the ice cream truck over getting a hundred thousand dollar car. They are hidden monkeys on our backs and unless we as a nation identify them we will be in for a rude awakening. The monkeys need to be identified in order to remove them, else you will multiply them onto your children and you will get what you give.

Acknowledgement

First, to give honor and gratefulness to my Lord and Saviour, Jesus Christ, for whom without I wouldn't have been able to give birth to this baby. His love enabled me to endure live pressures and circumstances that may have caused me at times to think of suicide on many occasions. I love you Lord and give my life back to you. I will forever work for you. To my mother who gave me physical life and the love that she was able to give. I appreciate all that you have taught me. You gave me the foundation and the faith in Jesus and the knowledge of his sacrifice for me. You gave me a home of Christ and fed my soul while keeping me from carnal knowledge the best way you knew how. She told me of my father's expectations for my life; that was the driving force in my education. I will forever love you. To my Raj, who became my father figure and taught me not to be gullible. Thank you for the many debates that exercised and strengthen my thinking. Karl, I still consider you daddy. To my other siblings, for giving me the workout of a lifetime. Because of you, I am strong because I learned to depend on my faith which allowed me to develop my guns for this journey. To Clarence, my first love who taught me how to drive the freeways, do laundry, to speak well, and how to handle myself in a crowd. You encouraged me to fight and was a good sparring partner for what I believe in and not to back down when times were tough. To my sister/friend, Erica, who grounded me not to be judgmental and taught me empathy towards others. You are truly my angel. To Karen, my spiritual sister friend who always had a good word ready when I was getting physically and mentally weak. You are truly my angel. To my husband, Nathaniel, who married me twice. You taught me perseverance and patience and was able to put up with me while I was identifying the Monkeys and never gave up on me. You are my Spiritual soldier and my partner for life. To my first born, Candace, who understood that she was the practice child for motherhood; you gave me strength to endure the pressures to give you a life I needed as a child. To Jennifer and Nathaniel, my Thanksgiving babies, who gave me the opportunity to enjoy motherhood; you taught me a lot about unconditional love and allowed me to mother you with respect and obedience. To Evan, I appreciate you taking the time to design my book cover and website; you are really heaven sent. To my In-laws, who I was giving the opportunity to learn submission and endurance with tough situations; I ain't mad at you. You taught me that family is family and they are to be accepted where they are and not where I want them to be. You and my family taught me how to be a true matriarch and role model to my children and grandchildren. And, last but not least, my coworkers throughout my life, you taught me a work ethic of a longtime.

God, the Father of us all, loved me even when I didn't love myself. Your sacrifice of your son offered me salvation and power that no one can take away from me. Thank you that you gave me the spiritual ears to hear and the spirit to accept it even when it hurt. I have been taught to accept the blessings you offered and I give my life to you. Now the mission begins, my faith is strong and I know that you will never leave me nor forsake me. To God be all the Glory. Amen!

www.ingramcontent.com/pod-product-compliance
Lightning Source LLC
Chambersburg PA
CBHW021218090426
42740CB00006B/267

* 9 7 8 0 6 1 5 6 4 1 6 0 7 *